Contents

AutoCAD Release 14

A CONCISE GUIDE

A Yarwood

LONGMAN

Addison Wesley Longman Limited
Edinburgh Gate, Harlow
Essex CM20 2JE, England
and Associated Companies throughout the world

First published 1999

British Library Cataloguing in Publication Data
A catalogue entry for this title is available from the British Library

ISBN 0-582-36873-1

Set by 24 in Times 10/12 and News Gothic
Produced by Addison Wesley Longman Singapore (Pte)
Printed in Singapore

CHAPTER 9

CHAPTER 10

CHAPTER 11

CHAPTER 12

CHAPTER 13

CHAPTER 14

Preface

This book is designed to be used as a course workbook for those wishing to learn how to operate the computer-aided design software package **AutoCAD Release 14**. Its pages contain a number of graded examples, worked examples and exercises suitable for those beginning to learn how to use the software for the production of technical drawings. The book's contents are suitable for use by a beginner working from home, for students at further and higher education colleges, or for those in industry wishing to learn how to operate the software.

The book is intended for use by those who have not had any experience using AutoCAD Release 14 and are coming new to working with the software. It is, however, assumed the reader has an elementary knowledge of working with a computer running the Windows 95 operating system.

AutoCAD Release 14 is a very complex software system and a book this size cannot possibly cover the complexities of all the methods of construction available. It is hoped however, that by the time the reader has worked through the contents of this book, they will have gained sufficient skill and knowledge to be able to go on to more advanced work, and will have gained an interest in the possibilities available when using the software for the construction of technical drawings.

My book *An Introduction to AutoCAD Release 14* published early in 1998 covers the use of the software in greater detail and can be regarded by those wishing to follow up on the skills gained by working through the course in this book as suitable reading for gaining further knowledge of the software.

A. Yarwood
Salisbury, 1998

Acknowledgements

The author wishes to acknowledge with grateful thanks the help given to him by members of the staff at Autodesk Ltd.

□ TRADEMARKS □

The following are registered in the US Patent and Trademark Office by Autodesk Inc.:

Autodesk, AutoCAD

IBM is a registered trademark of the International Business Machines Corporation.

MS-DOS is a registered trademark, and Windows a trademark of the Microsoft Corporation.

A. Yarwood is a Master Developer with Autodesk Ltd.

Registered Developer

CHAPTER 1

Terms and start up

Terms used throughout this book

- **Left-click**   Place the cursor under mouse control onto a feature and press the **Pick** button of the mouse. Shown in this book in italics: *'left-click'*.
- **Right-click**   Press the **Return** button of the mouse. Shown in this book in italics: *'right-click'*. The same result can be achieved by pressing the **Enter** or **Return** key of the keyboard.

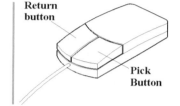

Return button

Pick Button

- **Double-click**   Place the cursor under mouse control onto a feature and press the **Pick** button of the mouse twice in rapid succession. Shown in this book in italics: *'double-click'*.
- **Drag**   Move the cursor under mouse control, hold down the **Pick** button and move the mouse. The feature moves with the mouse movement. Shown in this book in italics: *'drag'*.
- **Select**   Move the cursor onto a feature and press the **Pick** button of the mouse.
- **Pick**   The same action as *Select*. The two terms are used throughout this book and can be regarded as having the same meaning. Shown in this book in italics: *'pick'*.

Endpoint

- **Pick box**   An adjustable square associated with picking features of a construction.
- **Pick button**   The left-hand mouse button.
- **Enter**   Type the given word or letters at the keyboard.
- **Return**   Press the **Return** or **Enter** key of the keyboard. Usually, but not always, has the same result as a *right-click* – i.e. pressing the **Return** button of the mouse. Shown in this book in italics: *'Return'*.
- **Esc**   The **Esc** key of the keyboard. In Release 14 pressing the **Esc** key has the effect of cancelling the current action taking place.
- **Tab key**   The key usually on the left-hand side of the keyboard which carries two arrows.
- **Tool**   The name given to a command in recent releases of AutoCAD.
- **Icons**   A common feature in all Windows applications – a small graphic representing a tool or a function of the software in use.
- **Flyout**   A number of tool icons have a small arrow in the bottom right-hand corner of the icon. Such an icon will produce a 'flyout' of other icons when the cursor is placed over it and the **Pick** button of the mouse is held down.

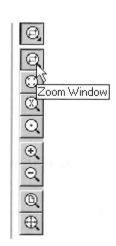

Zoom Window

- **Tool tip** The name of the tool represented by an icon, which appears when the mouse cursor is placed over a tool icon.
- **Default** The name given to the settings and parameters of an application as set automatically when the software is used for the very first time.
- **Objects** Individual lines, circles, etc. drawn in Release 14. When objects are collected together as a group or block the group is then treated as a single object.
- **Entity** Has the same meaning in Release 14 as 'object'.

Loading AutoCAD Release 14

When a computer running Windows 95 is switched on, after the operating software has loaded, the Windows 95 'desktop' appears. To load AutoCAD Release 14:

1 *Left-click* on the **Start** button.
2 *Left-click* on the **Programs** folder.
3 *Left-click* on the **AutoCAD R14** folder.
4 *Left-click* on the **AutoCAD R14** icon.

The Release 14 software then loads.

□ **NOTE** □

The **AutoCAD R14** shortcut icon may be on the Windows 95 desktop. If it is there, an easier method of loading Release 14 is to *double-click* on the shortcut.

The AutoCAD window

When the software files have loaded, the **Start Up** dialogue box appears. There are five buttons on the left-hand side of the dialogue box. *Left-click* on the **Use a Template** button, unless it has already been selected, when it will show highlighted (greyer than the other

buttons). In the list of drawing templates which appears (extension ***.dwt**) *double-click* on
Acadiso.dwt.

The main AutoCAD Release 14 window appears on screen.

The names of the parts of the Release 14 window are included in the illustration below. Note in particular that normally four toolbars are displayed by default. These are:

- The **Standard** toolbar.
- The **Object Properties** toolbar.
- The **Draw** toolbar.
- The **Modify** toolbar.

Most of the Release 14 window is taken up by the drawing area within which drawings are constructed.

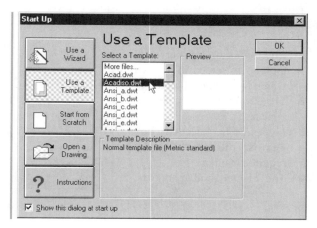

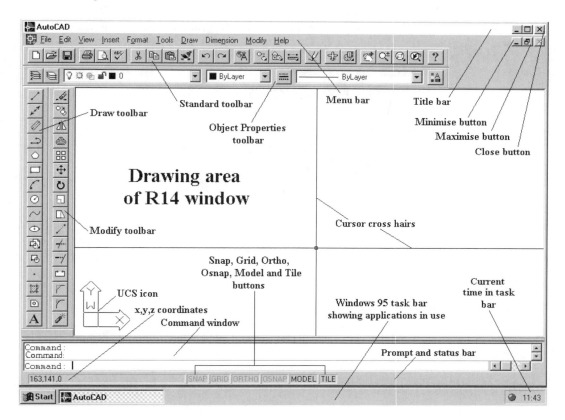

■ Toolbars

When first loaded the Release 14 window includes four toolbars. Other toolbars can be called:

1 *Right-click* in any part of a toolbar on screen in an area which is not part of an icon.
2 The **Toolbars** dialogue box appears.
3 *Left-click* in the check box against the name of the required toolbar.
4 The selected toolbar appears.

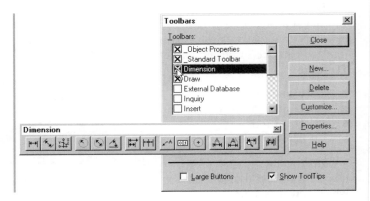

Toolbars can be **docked** on either side, or at the top or at the bottom of the Release 14 window. When away from the sides they are said to be **floating**, and can be resized using the cursor.

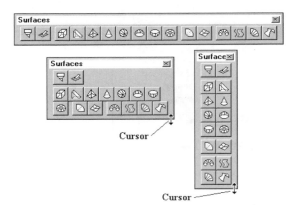

■ Dialogue boxes

Three types of boxes will be seen when operating Release 14: dialogue boxes, message boxes and warning boxes. The most important of these are the numerous dialogue boxes. These vary in appearance and the way in which they are laid out, but have common features some of which are shown opposite.

☐ **NOTE** ☐

If a question mark (**?**) within a small button is positioned at the top right of a dialogue box, a *left-click* on the button, followed by another on any part of the dialogue box, brings up a help box describing the function of that part of the dialogue box.

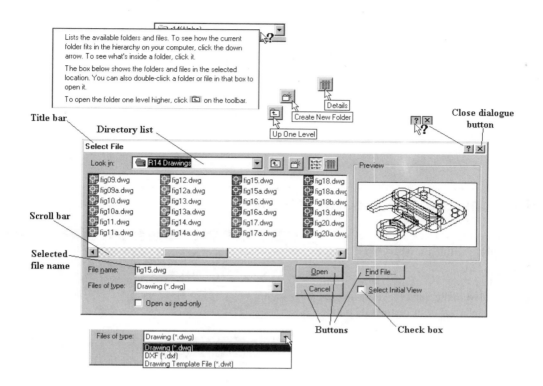

Lists the available folders and files. To see how the current folder fits in the hierarchy on your computer, click the down arrow. To see what's inside a folder, click it.

The box below shows the folders and files in the selected location. You can also double-click a folder or file in that box to open it.

To open the folder one level higher, click 🖻 on the toolbar.

Details

Create New Folder

Up One Level

Close dialogue button

Title bar

Directory list

Scroll bar

Selected file name

Buttons

Check box

The AutoCAD Help system

Help
AutoCAD Help Topics
Quick Tour
What's New
Learning Assistance
Connect to Internet
About AutoCAD

To call the **Help** system, *left-click* on **Help** in the menu bar and again on **AutoCAD Help Topics...** in the pull-down menu which appears. *Left-click* on the **Index** label and *enter* the name of the topic for which help is required in the **1 Type the first few letters of the word you're looking for** box. As an example *enter* **line**. *Left-click* on the **Display** button and a window appears showing help information for the **Line** tool.

Alternatively, when using any tool, press the **F1** key and a **Help** window for the tool in use appears. This form of help is 'associative' – it is associated with the tool being used at the time.

CHAPTER 2

Line and Polyline tools

Opening the acadiso.dwt template

Start up AutoCAD Release 14. Select **Use a Template** within the **Start Up** dialogue box.

Either *left-click* on the name **acadiso.dwt** in the **Select a Template** list, followed by a *left-click* on the **OK** button, or *double-click* on the name **acadiso.dwt**. The **acadiso.dwt** template appears.

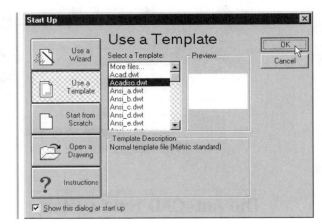

☐ **NOTE** ☐

Move the mouse and note that, as it moves, the coordinate figures in the left-hand end of the prompt and status bar change according to the position of the cursor. Note also that the figures are given to four decimals places.

For the time being we will be using the **acadiso.dwt** template layout for the construction of drawings. Later (Chapter 5) we will construct our own drawing template to use for most of the work contained in this book.

Drawing outlines by entering coordinate units

When constructing outlines with the **acadiso.dwt** template loaded, it can be assumed that each coordinate unit is equivalent to one millimetre. This is because the limits of this template are the same as the dimensions of an A4 sheet, which is a metric standard. There are two main methods of drawing outlines using coordinate units:

- **Entering absolute units**   The x,y coordinate position of each corner of the outline is *entered* in response to prompts at the Command Line.
- **Entering relative units**   The x,y coordinate distance between points on the outline is *entered* in response to prompts. Thus each new point is defined relative to the last point.

The Line tool

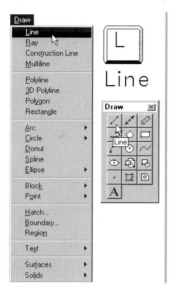

The **Line** tool can be called either by a *left-click* on its tool icon in the **Draw** toolbar, by *entering* **l** or **line** at the Command Line, or by selecting **Line** from the **Draw** pull-down menu. No matter which method is chosen, the prompts in the Command window are similar.

When the tool is called, the Command Line shows the prompts:

Command: _line
From point: the first point can be *picked* by moving the cursor under mouse control until it is in the required position, followed by a *right-click*. Or the *x,y* coordinate units of the first point can be *entered* by typing the numbers at the keyboard, followed by a *right-click*, or by pressing the **Return** key. The first prompt is then followed by the second prompt:
To point:

☐ **EXAMPLE 1** ☐ *using absolute coordinate entry*

Command: _line
From point: *enter* 100,200 *right-click*
To point: *enter* 250,200 *right-click*
To point: *enter* 250,150 *right-click*
To point: *enter* 300,150 *right-click*
To point: *enter* 300,100 *right-click*
To point: *enter* 250,100 *right-click*
To point: *enter* 250,40 *right-click*
To point: *enter* 100,40 *right-click*
To point: *enter* 100,100 *right-click*
To point: *enter* 150,100 *right-click*
To point: *enter* 150,150 *right-click*
To point: *enter* 100,150 *right-click*
To point: *enter* close *right-click*
Command:

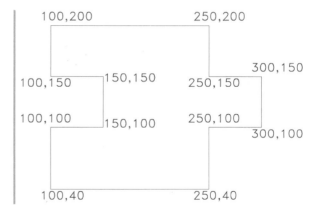

☐ **NOTES** ☐

1 Each time a new example is started, *left-click* on **File** in the menu bar, then on **New** in the dialogue box and *double-click* on **acadiso.dwt**.

2 If an error is made when *entering* figures, press **u** (for **Undo**). Pressing **u** repeatedly will eventually undo everything that has been done during a drawing session.

When using relative coordinate entry, the symbol @ must be placed before the *x,y* coordinate units of the distance between the *entered* point and the last point on the outline.

Command: _line
From point: *enter 90,245 right-click*
To point: *enter @120,0 right-click*
To point: *enter @0,-60 right-click*
To point: *enter @120,0 right-click*
To point: *enter @0,-40 right-click*
To point: *enter @-120,0 right-click*
To point: *enter @0,-20 right-click*
To point: *enter @-120,0 right-click*
To point: *enter c right-click*
Command:

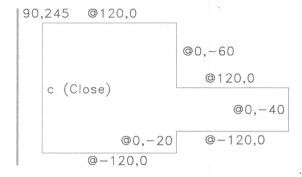

□ **NOTE** □

Some of the *x,y* coordinate units in this example are positive, some negative. Keep to the following conventions:

Positive x Horizontally to the right.
Positive y Vertically upwards.
Negative x Horizontally to the left.
Negative y Vertically downwards.

Command: _line
From point: *enter 140,220 right-click*
To point: *enter @100<45 right-click*
To point: *enter @100<315 right-click*
To point: *enter @50<330 right-click*
To point: *enter @50<210 right-click*
To point: *enter @100<225 right-click*
To point: *enter @100<135 right-click*
To point: *enter @50<150 right-click*
To point: *enter c right-click*
Command:

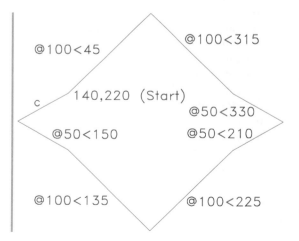

Angles in AutoCAD are measured anti-clockwise; the **positive x** coordinate direction is 0° by default. This means that in the 360 degrees of a circle, angles are measured as shown.

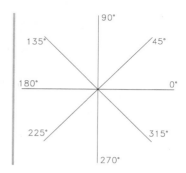

The Polyline tool

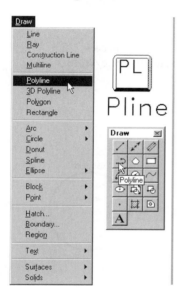

The **Polyline** tool can be called either by a *left-click* on its tool icon in the **Draw** toolbar, by *entering* **pl** or **pline** at the Command Line, or by selecting **Polyline** from the **Draw** pull-down menu. No matter which method is chosen, the prompts in the Command window are similar:

Command: _pline
From point: *pick* or *enter* coordinates
Arc/Close/Halfwidth/Length/Undo/Width/
 <Endpoint of line>:

Unless a simple straight polyline of zero width is required, it is necessary to respond by *entering* the initial letter of a command.

☐ **EXAMPLE 4** ☐ *pline outline of width 1*

Command: _pline
From point: *enter* 100,250 *right-click*
Arc/Close/Halfwidth/Length/Undo/Width/
 <Endpoint of line>: *enter* w *right-click*
Starting width <0>: *enter* 1 *right-click*
Ending width <1>: *right-click* (this accepts the default
 end width of 1)
Arc/Close/Halfwidth/Length/Undo/Width/
 <Endpoint of line>: *enter* 250,250 *right-click*

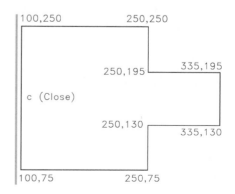

Arc/Close/Halfwidth/Length/Undo/Width/<Endpoint of line>: *enter* 250,195 *right-click*
Arc/Close/Halfwidth/Length/Undo/Width/<Endpoint of line>: *enter* 335,195 *right-click*
Arc/Close/Halfwidth/Length/Undo/Width/<Endpoint of line>: *enter* 335,130 *right-click*
Arc/Close/Halfwidth/Length/Undo/Width/<Endpoint of line>: *enter* 250,130 *right-click*
Arc/Close/Halfwidth/Length/Undo/Width/<Endpoint of line>: *enter* 250,75 *right-click*
Arc/Close/Halfwidth/Length/Undo/Width/<Endpoint of line>: *enter* 100,75 *right-click*
Arc/Close/Halfwidth/Length/Undo/Width/<Endpoint of line>: *enter* c *right-click*
Command:

☐ **EXAMPLE 5** ☐ *polyline arc*

Command: _pline
From point: *enter* 50,190 *right-click*
Arc/Close/Halfwidth/Length/Undo/Width/<Endpoint of line>: *enter* w *right-click*
Starting width <0>: *enter* 4 *right-click*
Ending width <4>: *right-click* (accepts the 4)
Arc/Close/Halfwidth/Length/Undo/Width/<Endpoint of line>: *enter* a *right-click*
**Angle/CEnter/CLose/Distance/Halfwidth/Line/Radius/Second point/Undo/Width/
    <Endpoint of arc>:** *enter* s (second point) *right-click*
Second point: *enter* 120,240 *right-click*
Endpoint of arc: *enter* 195,190 *right-click*
<Endpoint of arc>: *right-click*
Command: *right-click* (recalls Pline)
PLINE
From point: *enter* 280,185 *right-click*
Arc/Close/Halfwidth/Length/ Undo/Width/<Endpoint of line>: *enter* w *right-click*
Starting width <0>: *enter* 2 *right-click*

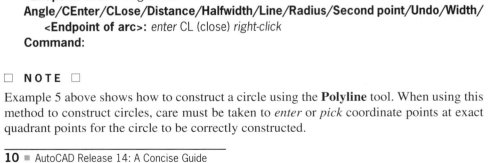

Ending width <2>: *right-click* (accepts the 2)
Arc/Close/Halfwidth/Length/Undo/Width/<Endpoint of line>: *enter* a *right-click*
**Angle/CEnter/CLose/Distance/Halfwidth/Line/Radius/Second point/Undo/Width/
    <Endpoint of arc>:** *enter* s (second point) *right-click*
Second point: *enter* 335,240 *right-click*
Endpoint of arc: *enter* 390,185 *right-click*
<Endpoint of arc>: *right-click*
**Angle/CEnter/CLose/Distance/Halfwidth/Line/Radius/Second point/Undo/Width/
    <Endpoint of arc>:** *enter* CL (close) *right-click*
Command:

☐ **NOTE** ☐

Example 5 above shows how to construct a circle using the **Polyline** tool. When using this method to construct circles, care must be taken to *enter* or *pick* coordinate points at exact quadrant points for the circle to be correctly constructed.

□ **EXAMPLE 6** □ *differing polyline widths*

Try creating the polylines shown here – follow the cordinates and line widths given.

□ **EXAMPLE 7** □ *directional construction*

When using either the **Line** or the **Polyline** tools, if the 'rubber band' joining the last *entered* point to the cursor is in the direction in which the line or pline is to be drawn, the required length can be *entered* at the Command Line (followed by a *right-click*) and the line or pline will be drawn to the specified length.

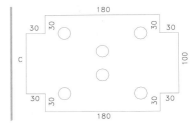

□ **NOTE** □

Leave Example 7 on screen and practise using the **Erase** tool.

The Erase tool

Erase is a tool which you will use frequently. There are several ways in which the tool can be used for deleting single objects or all the objects within a window, or deleting all objects crossed by a 'crossing window' selected with the mouse.

The **Erase** tool can be called either by a *left-click* on its tool icon in the **Modify** toolbar, by *entering* **e** or **erase** at the Command Line, or by selecting **Erase** from the **Modify** pull-down menu. No matter which method is chosen, the prompts in the Command window are similar.

The following examples demonstrate the use of the **Erase** tool.

□ **EXAMPLE 1** □

> **Command:** _erase
> **Select objects:** *pick* an object to be erased **1 found**
> **Select objects:** *pick* another object to be erased **1 found**
> **Select objects:** *right-click*
> **Command:** the *picked* objects are erased

□ **EXAMPLE 2** □

Command: _erase
Select objects: *enter* w (window) *right-click*
First corner: *pick* **Other corner:** *pick* **6 found** (the number of objectss found will depend on
    the area selected)
Select objects: *right-click*
Command: all objects within the window are erased

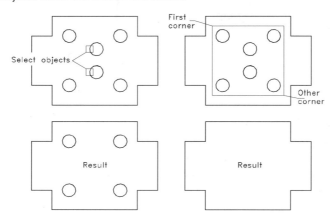

If the window is a crossing window (below), or if the **First corner:** is *picked* at the bottom right of the objects to be erased and the **Other corner:** is *picked* top left, all the objects **crossed** by the lines of the window are erased.

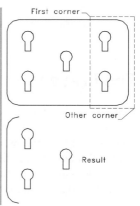

□ **EXAMPLE 3** □

Command: _erase
Select objects: *enter* c (crossing) *right-click*
First corner: pick **Other corner:** pick **7 found**
Select objects: *right-click*
Command: all objects crossed by the lines are erased

□ **EXAMPLE 4** □

Another method of erasing objects crossed by lines is to use a **fence**.

A response to **Select objects:** of **f** (fence) and objects crossed by the fence lines will be erased.

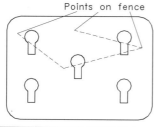
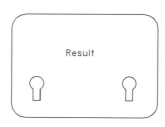

Object snaps

When an object snap (osnap) is in operation, the positioning of points in the construction of drawings can be made with precision. The technique allows the operator to construct drawings by accurately **snapping** entities to various parts of other entities – to ends, to midpoints, to the intersections of entities, etc. Object snaps can be set in a variety of ways, but the suggested method is to select them from the **Tracking** flyout; the icon is in the **Standard** toolbar by default. To select an osnap:

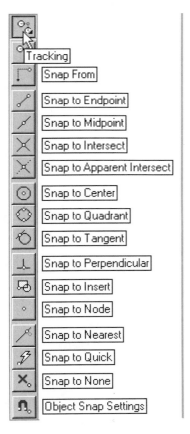

1 *Left-click* on the **Tracking** icon in the **Standard** toolbar. The **Object Snap** toolbar then appears as a flyout. The names (tool tips) of the many icons in the toolbar are shown.

2 When an osnap is called from the toolbar, a prompt appears in the prompt line showing its abbreviation. As an example, when the **Endpoint** osnap is selected from the toolbar, the prompt line shows:

_endp of

3 Osnaps only come into action when a drawing tool is in use. Selecting one at any other time brings up the error statement **Unknown command** at the Command window.

4 When an osnap is called a **pick box** appears at the intersection of the cursor hairs.

□ **NOTE** □

The abbreviations shown in the Command line are: **endp** – Endpoint; **mid** – Midpoint; **int** – Intersect; **cen** – Center; **qua** – Quadrant; **tan** – Tangent; **nod** – Node; **per** – Perpendicular.

□ **EXAMPLE 1** □

Examples are given of the use of the Endpoint, Midpoint, Intersection, Center and Quadrant osnaps. The **pick box** for each example is included in the relevant drawing.

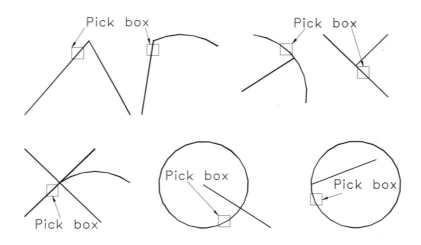

☐ **EXAMPLE 2** ☐

Examples are given in the use of the Tangent, Node and Nearest osnaps.

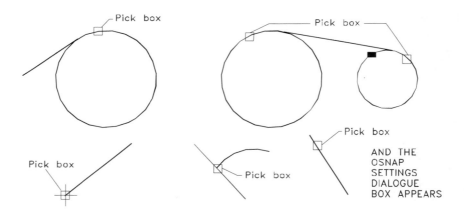

QUESTIONS

1 What is the difference between drawing using the absolute method of coordinate entry and the relative method?
2 Which is the default zero degree direction used for measurement of angles?
3 What is the purpose of using an **osnap**?
4 When using osnaps how can the size of the **pick box** be altered?
5 What is the advantage of having a **pick box** of a fairly large size when using osnaps?
6 Can you describe the use of the osnap **Snap From**?

---

7 What happens after a *left-click* on the **Object Snap Settings** icon?

8 How is a circle constructed with the aid of the **Polyline** tool?

9 How is an arrow constructed with the aid of the **Polyline** tool?

EXERCISES

Open the **acadiso.dwt** template. Construct the eight drawings following the coordinate units or dimensions given. Do not attempt adding dimensions at this stage; that comes later in this book. Use either the **Line** tool or the **Polyline** tool to complete the drawings; when using the **Polyline** tool, vary the width of the lines as indicated.

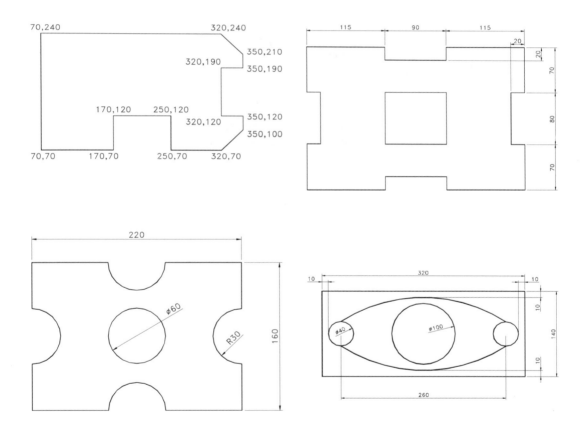

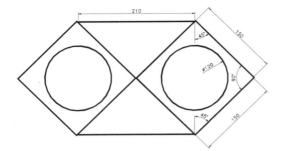

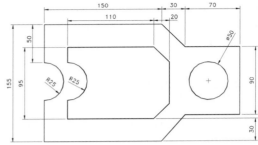

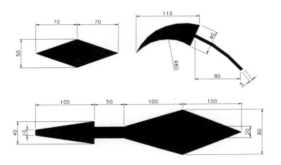

CHAPTER 3

AutoSnap and Draw tools

AutoSnap

With the **Osnap Settings** dialogue box on screen, *left-click* on the **AutoSnap(TM)** label. The **AutoSnap** dialogue box appears. Set all the check boxes in the **Select settings** area of the dialogue box 'on' (ticks in boxes). When osnaps are now used, the AutoSnap system comes into operation.

There are three parts of AutoSnap when it is set to be in action: a **marker**, a **magnet** and a **snap tip**.

1 If the marker is turned off no pick box appears with the AutoSnap.
2 If the magnet is turned off, AutoSnap does not lock to the nearest snap point.
3 If the snap tip is turned off the name of the osnap doesn't show when osnaps are used.

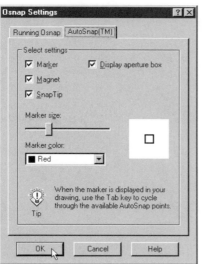

□ **NOTE** □

1 If several osnaps are set to 'on' in the **Osnaps Settings** dialogue box, when AutoSnap is active, pressing the **Tab** key will cycle through all the possible snap points in turn.

2 A different shape marker will show for each of the AutoSnap markers, depending upon which osnap is in use.

3 AutoSnap only functions for osnaps already selected or set.

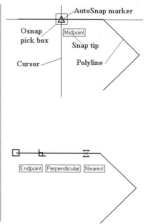

The Circle tool

To call the **Circle** tool, either *left-click* on the **Circle** tool icon in the **Draw** toolbar, or on **Circle** from the **Draw** pull-down menu, or *enter* **c** or **circle** at the Command Line. When calling the tool from the **Draw** pull-down menu a sub-menu appears from which command prompts can be selected (instead of selecting the commands at the Command Line).

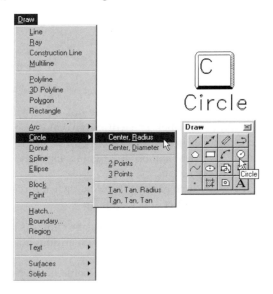

□ **EXAMPLE 1** □

> **Command:** _circle
> **CIRCLE 3P/2P/TTR/<Center point>:** *enter*
>   125,190 *right-click*
> **Diameter <Radius>:** *enter 70 right-click*
> **Command:** *right-click* (recalls circle)
> **CIRCLE 3P/2P/TTR/<Center point>:** *enter*
>   300,190 *right-click*
> **Diameter <Radius>:** *enter 50 right-click*
> **Command:**

If all osnaps and the AutoSnap feature have been set 'on' and lines drawn as shown, the osnap and AutoSnap **pick boxes**, snap tips and markers will show as each point is *picked* when drawing the lines.

If the AutoSnap feature is being used, it may be necessary to press the **Tab** key to cycle through the osnaps to obtain selections such as the **Center** marker.

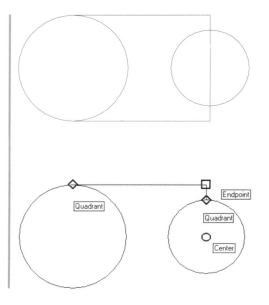

□ **EXAMPLE 2** □ *using the TTR prompt*

Command: _circle
CIRCLE 3P/2P/TTR/<Center point>: *enter* ttr *right-click*
Enter Tangent spec: *pick* one of the objects
Enter second Tangent spec: *pick* the other object
Radius: *enter* radius *right-click*
Command:

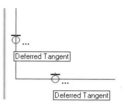

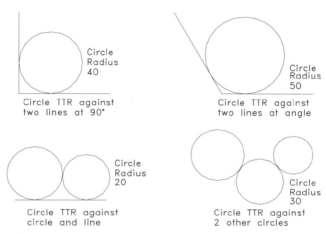

Circle Radius 40
Circle TTR against
two lines at 90°

Circle Radius 50
Circle TTR against
two lines at angle

Circle Radius 20
Circle TTR against
circle and line

Circle Radius 30
Circle TTR against
2 other circles

□ **EXAMPLE 3** □ *using the 3P and 2P prompts*

Command: _circle
CIRCLE 3P/2P/TTR/<Center point>: *enter* 3p *right-click*
First point: *enter* 110,230 *right-click*
Second point: *enter* 75,260 *right-click*
Third point: *enter* 25,260 *right-click*
Command: *right-click* (recalls Circle)
CIRCLE 3P/2P/TTR/<Center point>: *enter* 2p *right-click*
First point on diameter: *enter* 320,175
Second point on diameter: *enter* 425,120 *right-click*
Command:

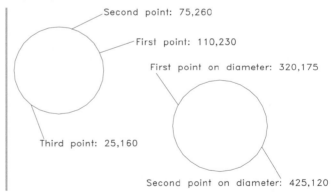

Second point: 75,260
First point: 110,230
First point on diameter: 320,175
Third point: 25,160
Second point on diameter: 425,120

The Arc tool

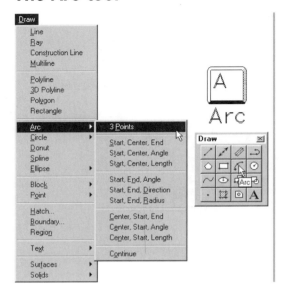

To call the **Arc** tool, either *left-click* on the **Arc** tool icon in the **Draw** toolbar, or on **Arc** from the **Draw** pull-down menu, or *enter* **a** or **arc** at the Command Line. When calling the tool from the **Draw** pull-down menu a sub-menu appears from which command prompts can be selected (instead of selecting commands at the Command Line).

The four examples shown below were all drawn after using the **Arc** sub-menu.

□ **NOTE** □

When drawing arcs they must be drawn anti-clockwise (counter-clockwise).

□ **EXAMPLE 1** □

Command: _arc Center/<Start point>: *pick* a point
Center/End/<Second point>: *pick* a point
End point: *pick* a point
Command:

□ **EXAMPLE 2** □

Command: _arc Center/<Start point>: *pick* a point
Center/End/<Second point>: _c Center *pick* a point
Angle/Length of chord/<End point>: *pick* a point
Command:

□ **EXAMPLE 3** □

Command: _arc Center/<Start point>: *pick* a point
Center/End/<Second point>: _a Included angle: *pick* a point
Angle/Length of chord/<End point>: *enter* degrees
Command:

□ **EXAMPLE 4** □

Command: _arc Center/<Start point>: *pick* a point
Center/End/<Second point>: _c Center *pick* a point
Angle/Length of chord/<End point>: _l Length of chord:
  enter a number (length)
Command:

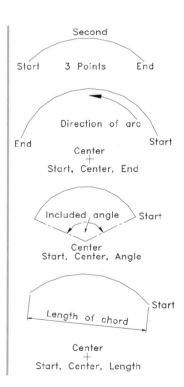

The Edit Polyline tool

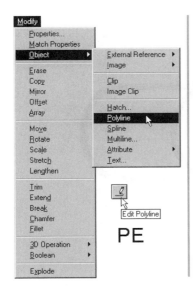

Polylines (plines) can be edited with the aid of the **Edit Polyline** tool, usually referred to as **Pedit**. To call **Pedit**, either select the tool from the **Modify II** toolbar, or **Polyline** from the **Object** sub-menu of the **Modify** pull-down menu, or *enter* **pe** at the Command Line. The most often used editing facilities are the changing of the width, the joining of adjacent polylines and the closing of open polylines. Try practising all the various command sequences.

Command: *enter* pe *right-click*
PEDIT Select polyline: *pick*
**Close/Join/Width/Edit vertex/Fit/Spline/
    Decurve/Ltype gen/Undo/eXit <X>:**

□ **EXAMPLE 1** □ *using the Width option*

Draw a rectangle with the aid of the **Polyline** tool as shown below.

Command: *enter* pe *right-click*
PEDIT Select polyline: *pick*
Close/Join/Width/Edit vertex/Fit/Spline/Decurve/Ltype gen/Undo/eXit <X>: *enter*
    w *right-click*
Enter new width for all segments: *enter* 2 (centre) or 6 (right) *right-click*
Open/Join/Width/Edit vertex/Fit/Spline/Decurve/Ltype gen/Undo/eXit <X>: *right-click*
Command:

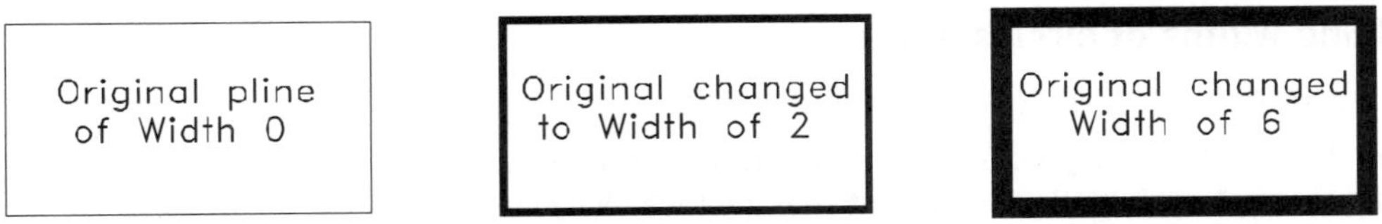

```
Original pline
of Width 0
```

```
Original changed
to Width of 2
```

```
Original changed
Width of 6
```

□ **EXAMPLE 2** □ *using the Join option*

Draw a polyline as shown below – two separate polyline arcs joined by two separate polylines.

Command: *enter* pe *right-click*
PEDIT Select polyline: *pick* one of the plines

Close/Join/Width/Edit vertex/Fit/Spline/Decurve/Ltype gen/Undo/eXit <X>: *enter* j *right-click*

Select objects: *window the whole outline* **3 found**

Select objects: *right-click* **3 segments added to polyline**

Open/Join/Width/Edit vertex/Fit/Spline/Decurve/Ltype gen/Undo/eXit <X>: *right-click*

Command:

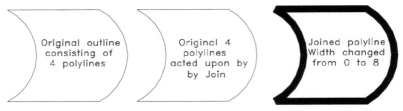

Original outline consisting of 4 polylines

Original 4 polylines acted upon by by Join

Joined polyline Width changed from 0 to 8

☐ **EXAMPLE 3** ☐ *using the Close (or Open) option*

Draw an open polyline as shown below (left-hand drawing).

Command: *enter* pe *right-click*

PEDIT Select polyline: *pick one of the plines*

Close/Join/Width/Edit vertex/Fit/Spline/Decurve/Ltype gen/Undo/eXit <X>: *enter* c *right-click*

Open/Join/Width/Edit vertex/Fit/Spline/Decurve/Ltype gen/Undo/eXit <X>: *right-click*

Command:

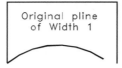
Original pline of Width 1

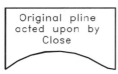
Original pline acted upon by Close

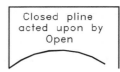
Closed pline acted upon by Open

Editing widths of circles and arcs

☐ **EXAMPLE 1** ☐ *changing the width of a circle*

A circle cannot be edited with the aid of **Pedit** without first changing it into an arc. This can be carried out with the aid of the **Break** tool which can be called from the **Modify** toolbar or by *entering* **br** at the Command Line. When using **Break** on a circle first *pick* the circle then *pick* a second point anti-clockwise from the first.

Break

Command: *enter* br *right-click*

BREAK Select object: *pick the circle*

Enter second point (or F for first point): *pick a point a little way anti-clockwise from the first*

Command:

Command: *enter* pe *right-click*
PEDIT Select polyline: *pick* the broken circle
Object selected is not a polyline
Do you wish to change it into one? <Y>: *right-click*
Close/Join/Width/Edit vertex/Fit/Spline/Decurve/Ltype gen/Undo/eXit <X>: *enter*
  w *right-click*
Enter new width for all segments: *enter* 2 *right-click*
Close/Join/Width/Edit vertex/Fit/Spline/Decurve/Ltype gen/Undo/eXit <X>: *enter*
  c *right-click*
Close/Join/Width/Edit vertex/Fit/Spline/Decurve/Ltype gen/Undo/eXit <X>: *right-click*
Command:

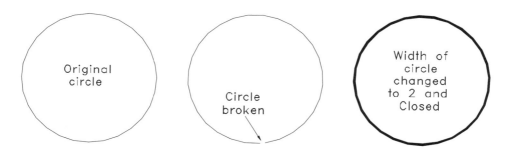

☐ **EXAMPLE 2** ☐ *changing the width of an arc*

When an arc is drawn with the aid of the **Arc** tool, it is not a polyline, so it must first be changed into one.

Command: *enter* pe *right-click*
PEDIT Select polyline: *pick* the broken circle
Object selected is not a polyline
Do you wish to change it into one? <Y>: *right-click*
Close/Join/Width/Edit vertex/Fit/Spline/Decurve/Ltype gen/Undo/eXit <X>: *enter*
  w *right-click*
Enter new width for all segments: *enter* 2 (centre) or 10 (right) *right-click*
Close/Join/Width/Edit vertex/Fit/Spline/Decurve/Ltype gen/Undo/eXit <X>: *enter*
  c *right-click*
Command:

---

1 What is the purpose of the **AutoSnap** system?
2 How is **AutoSnap** set up to work when constructing a drawing?
3 What is an AutoSnap **Marker**?
4 What action must precede the changing of the width of the outline of a circle?
5 What is the purpose of the **TTR** prompt of the Circle command prompt sequence?
6 What is the difference between drawing an arc using the **Polyline** tool and one using the **Arc** tool?
7 From which toolbar can the **Break** tool be selected?
8 Where would you usually be expected to find the toolbar from which **Break** can be selected?
9 What happens if, when using the **Break** tool, the second point is selected at a point clockwise from the first?
10 What is the purpose of the **Edit Polyline** tool?

EXERCISES

1 Construct the drawing below with lines of thickness of 0.7. Use **Pline**, **Circle** and **Pedit**.

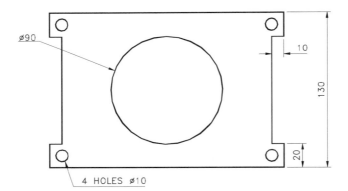

2 Draw the circles as shown, with the aid of the **TTR** prompt of the **Circle** Command sequence.

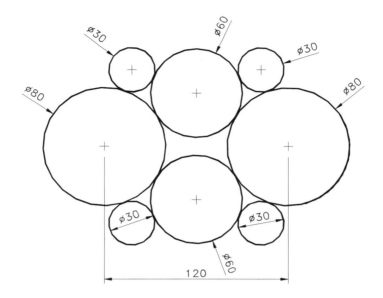

3 Construct the drawing, using a line width of 1, with the **Polyline** tool.

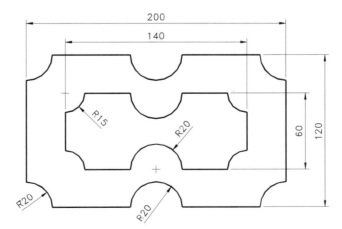

4 Construct the drawing below with the aid of the **Polyline**, **Circle** and **Edit Polyline** tools. Change the width of all lines to 0.7.

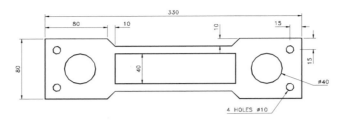

5 The drawing on the left shows two parts of a trolley arrangement. The drawing on the right shows the outline of one of the parts.

Using the **Polyline** tool, construct the outline to the dimensions given.

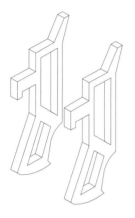

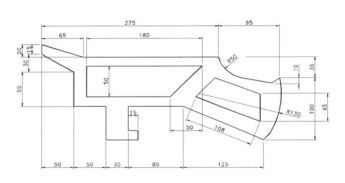

6 The drawing below shows a view of two bobbins on a spindle. A section through one of the bobbins is included.

    Ignoring the hidden detail, construct an accurate copy of the spindle and the two bobbins working with the **Polyline** and **Arc** tools and using a line width of 1.

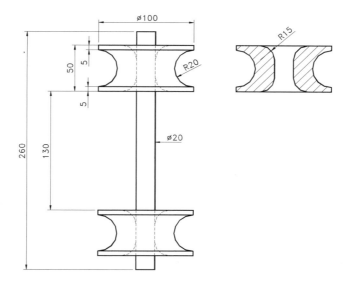

7 The drawing below is a front view of a machine handle. Using the **Polyline** and **Arc** tools construct an accurate copy of the view. Do not include any of the centre lines.

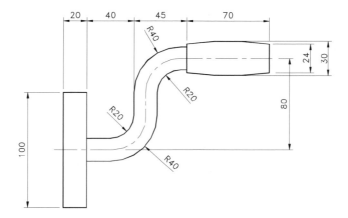

☐ **NOTE** ☐

Do not include any of the dimensions with your drawing answers. Adding dimensions to a drawing will be discussed later in this book.

CHAPTER 4

AutoCAD basics

Saving your work

When working through this book, particularly when constructing answers to exercises, it is best to save your constructions on a floppy disk; you can then keep them and can reload drawings as and when necessary.

AutoCAD drawings are saved with the file extension ***.dwg**. When using the **Save As...** tool from the **File** pull-down menu, it is not necessary to include the file extension with the name being *entered* in the **File name:** box of the **Save Drawing As** dialogue box. The extension is added automatically.

You are advised to save any work being constructed at regular intervals, say every fifteen minutes, to avoid loss of work if something goes wrong – loss of power to the computer, a software crash (very unusual with Release 14) or for any other reason. If you are satisfied that the file name under which a drawing is being saved is correct, it is easiest to use the **Save** command from the **File** pull-down menu. Just *left-click* on the name and the drawing will be saved automatically without having to use the **Save Drawing As** dialogue box.

The Zoom tools

The set of **Zoom** tools are important. They are among the most frequently used tools when working within AutoCAD. The easiest method of zooming a part of a drawing is to *enter* **z** at the Command Line, followed by *entering* the initial letter of the zoom command required.

> **Command:** *enter z right-click*
> **All/Center/Dynamic/Extents/Previous/Scale (X/XP)/Window/<Realtime>:**

The three most frequently used of these methods of zooming are **Realtime**, **Window** and **Previous**. In effect, **Realtime** and **Window** have the same results, in that a portion of the drawing to be zoomed is made to fill the drawing area of the AutoCAD window. Using the **Previous** zoom takes the drawing back to the prior zoom setting. You are advised to practise with the other **Zoom** commands in order to understand how they function.

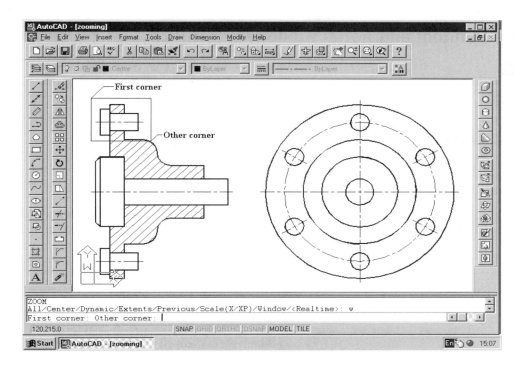

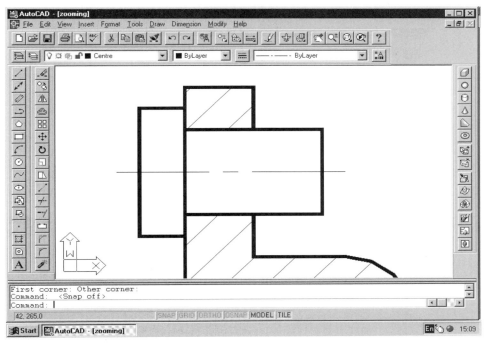

The Pan tool and Aerial window

Left-click on **Aerial View** in the **View** pull-down menu. The **Aerial View Window** appears in the bottom right corner of the AutoCAD window. It shows a miniature view of the full drawing area, and the part of the drawing on screen is enclosed by a thick black line. The **Aerial View** window is of particular value when working with large drawings in screens with **Limits** set to large numbers, because it shows clearly the part of the whole drawing which is being worked on at any time.

Call the **Pan** tool by *entering* **p** at the Command Line:

Command: *enter* p *right-click* and a 'hand' icon appears on screen.
Press Esc or Enter to exit, or right-click to activate pop-up menu

Moving the icon with the mouse moves the drawing in the direction in which the hand is moved. This allows the operator to work in areas not currently on screen. *Right-click* and a popup menu appears. *Left-click* on **Exit** in this menu and the panning sequence ends. The black rectangle in the **Aerial View Window** moves in response showing which part of the drawing is now on screen. When zooming, the black rectangle also shows the area zoomed on screen.

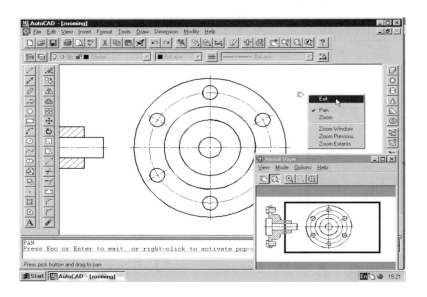

EXERCISES

1 Load one of the drawing exercises you completed from Chapter 2 and practise using the **Zoom** tools on your drawing.

Also try **Zoom Window, Zoom All, Zoom Previous, Zoom Scale, Zoom Dynamic** and **Zoom Center**.

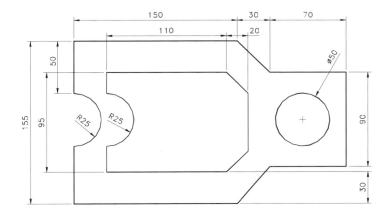

2 Using the same drawing, practise using the **Pan** tool.

3 With the same drawing on screen, call the **Aerial View** window and practise using the **Zoom** and **Pan** tools, noting the results in the **Aerial Zoom** window as you do so.

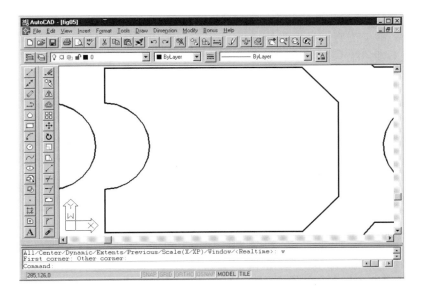

CHAPTER 5

AutoCAD 14 templates

Practically all the drawings in this book have been drawn in an AutoCAD Release 14 drawing window set up as a template. Once this set up has been completed, it is advisable to save it on disk as an AutoCAD drawing template. AutoCAD drawing templates have the file extension *.dwt. Throughout the remainder of this book the file name given to this drawing template is **yarwood.dwt** – my name followed by the template extension **dwt**.

Settings

This template includes the following settings:

- **Limits**   Set to **420,297** – the dimensions of an A4 sheet in millimetres.
- **Units**   Set to **0** figures after the decimal point.
- **Drawing Aids**   **Grid** spacing set to **10**, **Snap** set to **5**, **Blips** set on or off as desired.
- **Text Style**   Set to **Romand**, height **6**.
- **Dimension Style**   As shown on page 34 of this chapter.
- **Layers**   Setting the layers:
  0   The default AutoCAD layer on which outlines are drawn.
  Centre   The layer on which centre lines are drawn.
  Construction   The layer on which construction lines are drawn.
  Dimensions   The layer on which dimensions are drawn.
  Hidden   The layer on which hidden lines are drawn.
  Text   The layer on which text is drawn.

Limits

Left-click on **Format** in the menu bar, followed by another *left-click* on **Drawing Limits**. At the Command Line, the following appears:

    Command: _limits
    Reset Model Space limits:
    ON/OFF <Lower left corner> <0,0>: *right-click* (to accept 0,0)
    Upper right corner <420,297>: *right-click* (to accept 420,297)
    Command:

■ Units

1 *Left-click* on **Units...** in the **Format** pull-down menu.
   The **Units Control** dialogue box appears on screen.
2 In the dialogue box, *left-click* in the box under the word **Precision:** and again on **0** in the popup list which appears.
3 *Left-click* on the **OK** button.

This sets the number of figures after the decimal point when figures are entered in the drawing area to none.

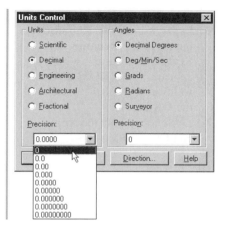

■ Drawing Aids

1 *Left-click* on **Tools** in the menu bar. In the pull-down menu *left-click* on **Drawing Aids....** The **Drawing Aids** dialogue box appears.
2 In the dialogue box, click in the **Snap** and in the **Grid** check boxes to set them 'on' (ticks in the boxes).
3 *Enter* **5** in the **X Spacing** of **Snap** and **10** in the **X Spacing** of **Grid**.
4 *Left-click* on the **OK** button.

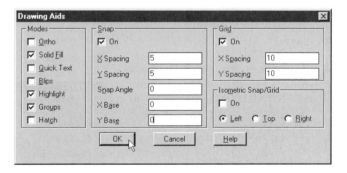

■ Text Style

1 *Left-click* on **Format** in the menu bar and again on **Text Style...** in the pull-down menu. The **Text Style** dialogue box appears.
2 In the dialogue box, *click* on **New**. The name **Style1** appears in the **Font Style** box.
3 *Left-click* on the **OK** button.
4 Select **romand.shx** from the **Font Name:** popup list.

5 *Enter* **6** in the **Height:** box.

6 *Left-click* on the **Rename** button in the **Rename Text Style** dialogue which appears, *enter* **ROMAND**, followed by a *left-click* on the **OK** button.

7 *Left-click* on both the **Apply** and **Close** buttons.

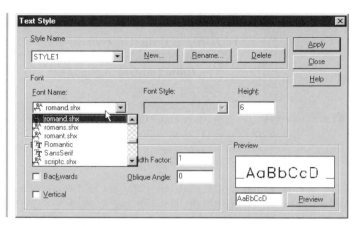

■ Dimension Style

1 At the Command Line *enter* **d** and *right-click*. The **Dimension Style** dialogue box appears.

2 Bring down the popup list in the **Current** box and make **STANDARD** the current style.

3 *Left-click* on the **Rename** button and rename the name **STANDARD** in the popup list to one of your own choice. I chose **MY_STYLE**.

4 *Left-click* on the **Geometry...** button. The **Geometry** dialogue box appears.

5 Make entries in the various parts of the **Geometry** dialogue box as shown. *Left-click* on the **OK** button.

6 *Left-click* on the **Format...** button. The **Format** dialogue box appears.

7 Make entries in the various parts of the **Format** dialogue box as shown. *Left-click* on the **OK** button.

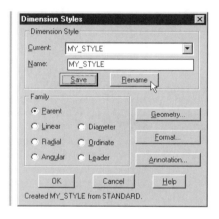

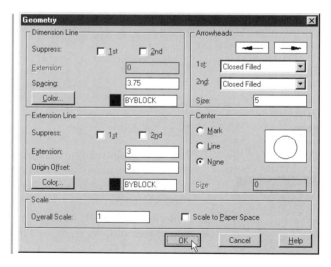

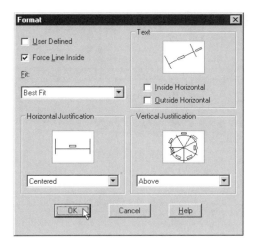

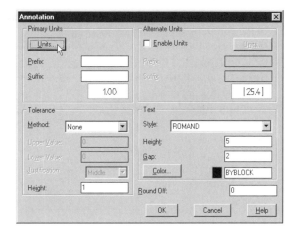

8 *Left-click* on the **Annotation...** button. The **Annotation** dialogue box appears.

9 Make entries in the **Annotation** dialogue box as shown.

10 While in the **Annotation** dialogue box, *left-click* on the **Units...** button. The **Primary Units** dialogue box appears.

11 Make settings in the **Primary Units** dialogue box as shown.

12 *Left-click* on the **OK** buttons of the **Primary Units**, the **Annotation** and the **Dimension Style** dialogue boxes in turn. The correct dimension style is now set.

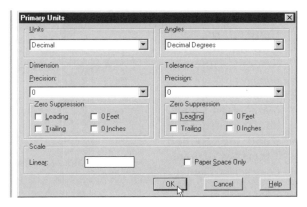

■ Layers

1 *Left-click* on the **Layers** tool icon in the **Object Properties** toolbar. The **Layer & Linetype Properties** dialogue box appears.

2 *Left-click* on the **New** button five times to create five new layers, **Layer1** to **Layer5**.

3 *Left-click* on each layer name in turn and overwrite the names for layers to:

Centre
Construction
Dimensions
Hidden
Text

4 *Double-click* on one of the colour boxes on the right of the layer descriptions. The **Select Color** dialogue box appears. A colour for a layer can be set with a *double-click* on the colour required for each layer. Change the colours for two layers:

Centre – blue
Hidden – red

5 *Double-click* on the **Centre** layer name **Continuous**. The **Select Linetype** dialogue box appears. In the dialogue box, *left-click* on **Load...** and then from the **Load or Reload Linetypes** dialogue box, select **Center2** and *left-click* on **OK**. Then select **Hidden2** and *left-click* on **OK**.

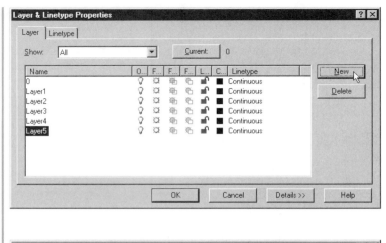

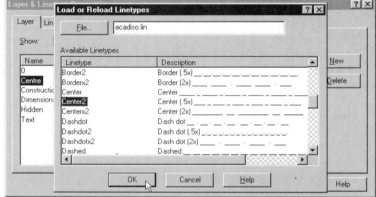

Allocate the **Center2** linetype to layer **Centre** and **Hidden2** to layer **Hidden**.

6 Your layers have now been set. If the **Layer Control** dialogue box is recalled (*left-click* on the **Layers** tool icon) it may be seen that another layer, **Defpoints**, has been automatically added.

Checking the linetype scale

When AutoCAD is first opened, the linetype scale will normally be set at 1. It is however advisable to check this when setting up your template file. To check the scale:

1 At the Command Line:

Command: *enter* ltscale *right-click*
New scale factor (1.0000): *right-click*
Command:

2 If however the linetype scale shows at any other figure, then:

Command: *enter* Itscale *right-click*
New scale factor (2.0000): *enter* 1 *right-click*
Command:

The linetype scale will now be set at 1. This means in effect that when constructing drawings in your drawing template each coordinate unit (see page 38) will be equivalent to 1mm when the drawing is printed or plotted (see page 129). This means that when printed or plotted at full scale (1:1) a line that is, say, 15 coordinate units long will be 15 mm long on paper.

Saving the template file

1 *Left-click* on **File** in the menu bar and, in the pull-down menu, *left-click* on **Save As….** The **Save Drawing As** dialogue box appears.

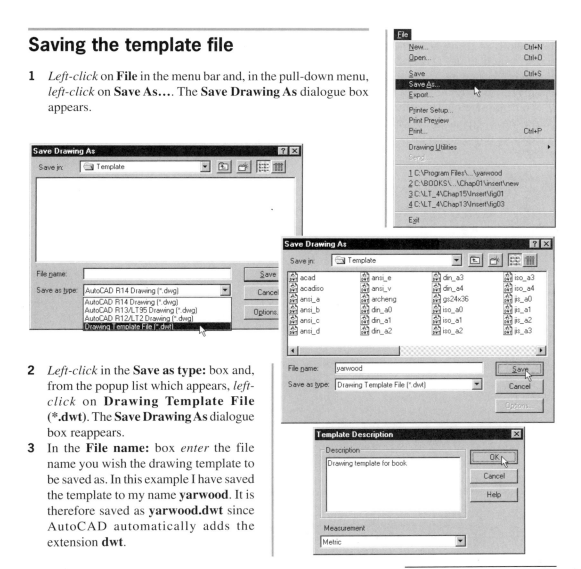

2 *Left-click* in the **Save as type:** box and, from the popup list which appears, *left-click* on **Drawing Template File (*.dwt).** The **Save Drawing As** dialogue box reappears.

3 In the **File name:** box *enter* the file name you wish the drawing template to be saved as. In this example I have saved the template to my name **yarwood**. It is therefore saved as **yarwood.dwt** since AutoCAD automatically adds the extension **dwt**.

4 *Left-click* on the **Save** button. The **Template Description** dialogue box appears. In the **Description** box enter a suitable description for your template.

5 Next time you load AutoCAD, you will be able to select your template prior to commencing a work session.

The AutoCAD coordinate units system

Drawings are constructed in AutoCAD in either a (2D) two-dimensional system or in a three-dimensional system (3D). When working in 2D the coordinates are expressed in terms of x and y. The x units measure horizontally; the y units vertically. With this system, any point in the window can be referred to in terms of x,y. Thus the point $x,y = 70,40$ is 70 units horizontally to the right of the origin (where $x,y = 0,0$) and 40 units vertically above the origin. A number of 2D coordinate points are shown below.

Coordinate points can be measured in negative figures. Thus the point $x,y = -100,-50$ is a point 100 units to the left of the origin and 50 units below it.

Three-dimensional coordinates include a third coordinate – the z coordinate. The positive z direction is perpendicularly out of the screen, towards the operator; the negative z direction is therefore directly into the screen, away from the operator.

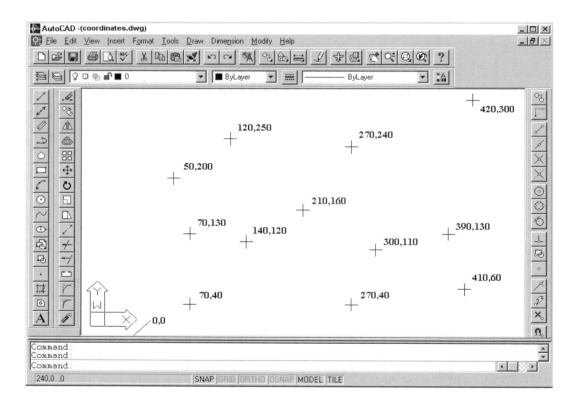

□ **NOTE** □

The coordinate reading in the status line always shows three coordinates, e.g. $x,y,z = 70,40,0$, even if you only use 2D coordinates. If you do not specify a z coordinate, it is assumed to be zero.

□ **NOTE** □

Press the two keys **Ctrl** and **D** together, and note what happens to the coordinates showing in the status bar. Now press the two keys again. The figures change from showing absolute units to relative units to showing none. There is more about absolute and relative coordinate units in Chapter 2.

Saving your work

At this stage it is as well to start saving all your drawings on floppy disks of your own.

In many of the chapters of this book, the chapter ends with a series of exercises. When you work through these, it is a good idea to save the results on your personal floppy disk. This will enable you to open any of your own drawings later in order to add, say, dimensions, or to recall at what stage you learned some new operation.

Save each exercise answer within a directory named to match the relevant chapter – for example:

Chap01/exercise_03
Chap02/exercise_06

■ Saving your template file

It is also a good idea to save your template file to your own floppy disk. This saves confusion when others using the same computer are opening a drawing template, and lets you use your template file on other computers.

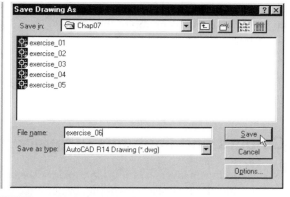

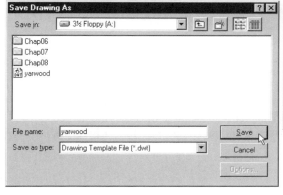

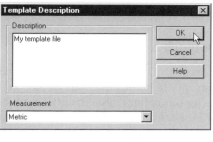

CHAPTER 6

Layers

The use of layers is an important concept when using any computer-aided design (CAD) package such as AutoCAD Release 14.

Layers can be imagined as being similar to tracings used when drawing 'by hand'. Tracings are constructed to lie on top of each other.

- Tracing can be removed; layers can be turned off or 'frozen'.
- Tracings can be replaced in a sequence; layers can be turned back on or 'thawed'.
- When a tracing is on top of the others, it can be drawn on; constructions can be added to the current layer in an AutoCAD drawing.

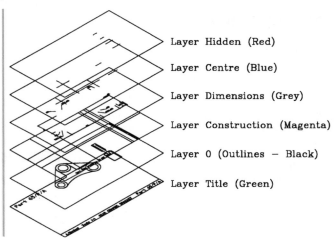

Layer Hidden (Red)

Layer Centre (Blue)

Layer Dimensions (Grey)

Layer Construction (Magenta)

Layer 0 (Outlines – Black)

Layer Title (Green)

Colours and linetypes in layers

When working on layers it is advisable to draw the constructions on each layer in a different colour. This makes for easier working because the operator can determine by colour alone which layer is being worked on. Layers may also have different linetypes.

■ Linetypes

A large number of different linetypes are stored in the file **acadiso.lin**. The drawings in this book use only three of these many linetypes. These are **Continuous** (for outlines, etc.), **Centre** (for centre lines through the centres of circles, cylinders, arcs, etc.) and **Hidden** (to show hidden parts in a drawing). As was seen in Chapter 5, these three linetypes are named **Continuous**, **Center2** and **Hidden2** and are loaded from the **Load or Reload Linetypes** dialogue box (see page 36).

Linetypes in technical drawings

In general most mechanical engineering technical drawings are made up from these types of lines. In other types of drawings, such as those for building and architecture, many other types of lines may be used.

An example of a technical drawing

The drawing below was constructed on the layers set up in Chapter 5 (page 35). The drawing is a two-view orthographic projection of a gear change bracket using the types of lines as shown above.

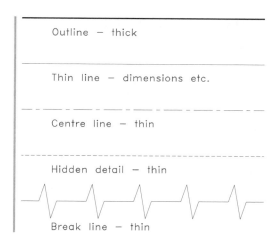

Outline — thick

Thin line — dimensions etc.

Centre line — thin

Hidden detail — thin

Break line — thin

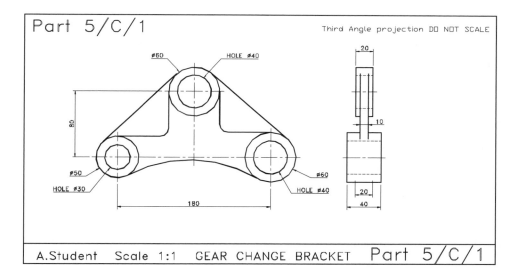

The Layer Control popup list

Left-click on the arrow on the right of the **Layer Control** box and its popup list appears. This shows the layers in the **yarwood.dwt** template described in Chapter 5. Against each layer name a number of icons appear, together with small squares coloured according to the colour allocated to the named layer.

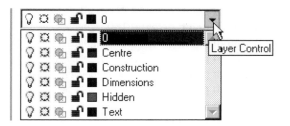

■ The Layer Control icons

The icons in the **Layer Control** popup list represent the items as shown. A *left-click* on the **On/Off** icon changes its colour from yellow to black (when black that layer is 'off'). A second *left-click* and the layer is turned on again. Similarly *left-clicks* on the other icons toggle the **Freeze/Thaw** and **Lock/Unlock** operations.

When a layer is locked, no modifying of objects already drawn on that layer can be made, although objects can be added to the locked layer.

When a layer is turned off or frozen it cannot be brought on screen.

A *left-click* on a layer name makes that layer the current layer on which constructions can be made.

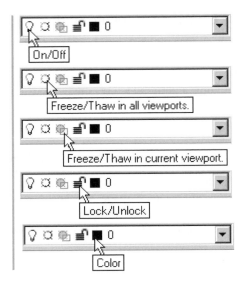

Construction lines

The **Construction Line** tool can be called either with a *left-click* on its icon in the **Draw** toolbar, by a *left-click* on its name in the **Draw** pull-down menu, or by *entering* **xl** at the Command Line.

> **Command:** *enter* xl *right-click*
> **XLINE Hor/Ver/Ang/Bisect/Offset/<From point>:**

Construction lines are of infinite length.

□ **EXAMPLE 1** □ *a drawing based on construction lines*

1 Open your drawing template.
2 *Left-click* on the arrow on the right of the **Layer Control** box in the popup list. *Left-click* on the name **Construction** in the list. This makes the **Construction** layer the current layer on which drawing can commence.
3 **Command: _xline Hor/Ver/Ang/Bisect/Offset/<From point>:** *enter* h *right-click*
Through point: *enter* 50,250 *right-click*
Through point: *enter* 50,160 *right-click*
Through point: *enter* 50,140 *right-click*
Through point: *enter* 50,100 *right-click*
Through point: *enter* 50,80 *right-click*
Through point: *enter* 50,20 *right-click*
Through point: *right-click*
Command: *right-click*

Command: _xline Hor/Ver/Ang/Bisect/Offset/
  <From point>: *enter* v *right-click*
Through point: *enter 50,160 right-click*
Through point: *enter 95,160 right-click*
Through point: *enter 105,160 right-click*
Through point: *enter 150,160 right-click*
Through point: *enter 190,160 right-click*
Through point: *enter 150,160 right-click*
Through point: *enter 270,160 right-click*
Through point: *right-click*
Command:

4 *Left-click* on **0** in the **Layer Control** popup list. This makes layer **0** the current layer.
5 Draw the outlines of the three views based upon the previously drawn construction lines, with the aid of the **Polyline** tool with **Width** set to **0.7**.

  Make use of the Intersect **osnap** or set **Snap** to **5** and 'on' to make the exact positioning of plines correct.

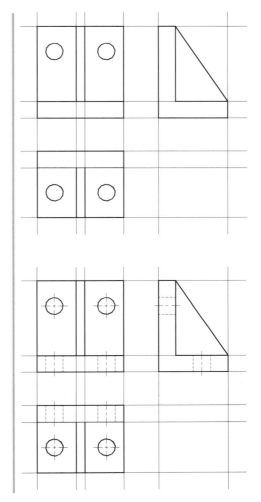

6 Make the layer **Centre** the current layer. Draw centre lines through each of the circles in all three directions.
7 Make the layer **Hidden** the current layer and draw hidden detail lines as necessary.
8 Turn off the layer **Construction**.

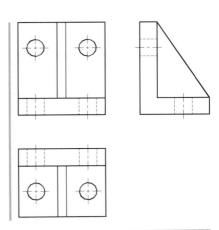

A pictorial view of a part from a machine is shown. This example describes the drawing of a two-view orthographic projection of the part.

1 Open your drawing template.
2 In the AutoCAD drawing window which appears the layer **0** will automatically be the current layer.
3 On layer **0**, and using the tools **Line**, **Arc** and **Circle**, or using the **Polyline** tool, construct the two views as shown. Work to the given sizes, but make no attempt to include the dimensions. If you are using the **Polyline** tool, you can, if you wish, draw the plines at a **Width** of 0.7.
4 In the popup list from the **Layer Control** box, *left-click* on **Centre** to make the layer **Centre** the current layer.
5 Add centre lines to the two views as required.
6 In the popup list from the **Layer Control** box, *left-click* on **Hidden** to make the layer **Hidden** the current layer.
7 Add hidden detail lines to the two views as required.
8 The completed drawing is as shown.

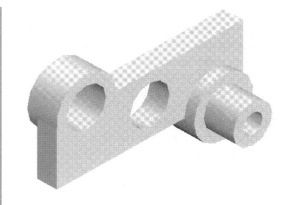

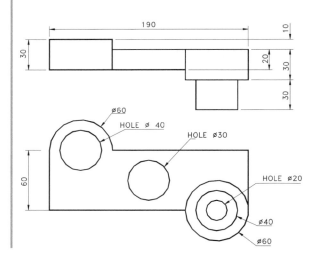

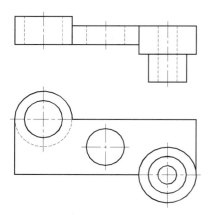

□ **EXAMPLE 3** □ *directional drawing*

There is another way of drawing lines and plines to accurate lengths. As an example:

Command: _line From point: *enter* 100,100 *right-click*
To point: move the cursor to the right horizontally *enter* 150 *right-click*
To point: move the cursor vertically upwards *enter* 120 *right-click*
To point: move the cursor to the left horizontally *enter* 150 *right-click*
To point: *enter* c *right-click*
Command:

A rectangle 150 by 120 units has been constructed (not illustrated).

□ **EXAMPLE 4** □ *part of an assembly*

When constructing any drawing, it will often be necessary to work out positions of points on lines, plines, arcs, centres of circles, etc. arithmetically on scrap paper before commencing the drawing. The operator may also find laying out a grid of construction lines of value (as shown in the first example on page 42). In this example, positions of some points have been worked out by arithmetic beforehand.

A pictorial view of the assembly is shown. It is the lower part only of this assembly to which this example refers.

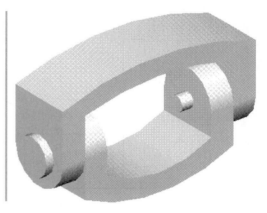

1 Open your drawing template.
2 **Command:** *enter* pl *right-click*
 From point: *enter* 90,250 *right-click*
 Arc/Close/Halfwidth/Length/
  Undo/Width/<Endpoint of
  line>: *enter* w *right-click*
 Starting width <0>: *enter* 0.7 *right-click*
 Ending width <0.7>: *right-click*
  (accepts 0.7)
 Arc/Close/Halfwidth/Length/
  Undo/Width/<Endpoint of
  line>: *enter* 90,250 *right-click*
 Arc/Close/Halfwidth/Length/
  Undo/Width/<Endpoint of line>: *enter* 120,250 *right-click*
 Arc/Close/Halfwidth/Length/Undo/Width/<Endpoint of line>: *enter* 120,180 *right-click*
 Arc/Close/Halfwidth/Length/Undo/Width/<Endpoint of line>: *enter* a *right-click*
 <Endpoint of arc>: *enter* s *right-click*
 Second point: *enter* 190,160 *right-click*
 End point: *enter* 260,180 *right-click*
 Angle/CEnter/CLose/Direction/Halfwidth/Line/Radius/Second point/Undo/Width/
  <Endpoint of arc>: *enter* l *right-click*
 Arc/Close/Halfwidth/Length/Undo/Width/<Endpoint of line>: *enter* 260,250 *right-click*
 Arc/Close/Halfwidth/Length/Undo/Width/<Endpoint of line>: *enter* 290,250 *right-click*

Arc/Close/Halfwidth/Length/Undo/Width/<Endpoint of line>: *enter* 290,160 *right-click*
Arc/Close/Halfwidth/Length/Undo/Width/<Endpoint of line>: *enter a right-click*
<Endpoint of arc>: *enter* s *right-click*
Second point: *enter* 190,135 *right-click*
End point: *enter* 90,160 *right-click*
Angle/CEnter/CLose/Direction/Halfwidth/Line/Radius/Second point/Undo/Width/
   <Endpoint of arc>: *enter* l *right-click*
Arc/Close/Halfwidth/Length/Undo/Width/<Endpoint of line>: *enter* c *right-click*
Command:

3   The outline of the front view of the part has now been completed. This may seem a somewhat long-winded process, but as your skill using AutoCAD increases, you will find that such sequences can be *entered* at the keyboard quite speedily.

4   Construct the end view and plan using the same techniques as for the front view – i.e. with the **Polyline** tool (or **Line** and **Arc** tools if preferred). The start points and other points in the two outlines will need to be worked out arithmetically, although using the **directional drawing** method may shorten the procedures.

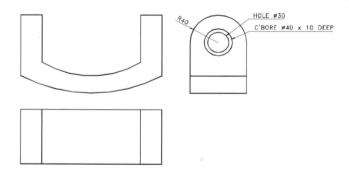

5   Make the layer **Centre** the current layer and with the aid of the **line** tool add all centre lines.
6   Make the layer **Hidden** the current layer and with the aid of the **line** tool add all hidden detail lines. The final drawing is as shown here.

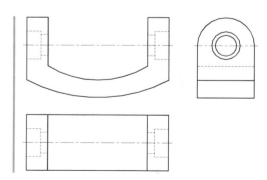

□ **NOTES** □

1 If an error has been made while *entering* the coordinate numbers, *enter* **u** (for **Undo**) and the last line or arc will be undone, allowing the correct figures to be *entered*.

2 The outline could have been drawn using the **Line** and **Arc** tools if desired.

3 The dimensions in the end view in the drawing below are included for guidance only. Do not try to include dimensions at this stage. Methods of adding dimensions to a drawing will be shown on pages 99 to 103.

QUESTIONS

1 Can you explain the purpose of using **layers** when constructing drawings in AutoCAD?

2 How are **colours** allocated to layers?

3 Can you list the settings you have made in order to produce a suitable drawing template file for your own use?

4 Why is it sensible to save this template file to a floppy disk which only you use?

5 Which do you personally prefer when drawing outlines of a drawing: polylines or lines?

6 What happens when a layer is turned **off**?

7 What is the purpose of **freezing** a layer?

8 When would a layer be **locked** and why?

9 When would you use **construction lines**?

10 What is meant by **directional drawing**?

EXERCISES

1 With the tools **Polyline**, **Circle** and **Arc** construct the three-view orthographic projection of the upper part of the assembly illustrated on page 45. Construct the three views using procedures similar to those used for constructing Example 4 on page 45. Do not attempt adding dimensions at this stage.

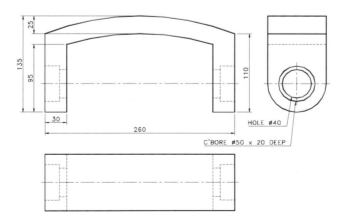

2 The upper line of drawings on the right show the parts of the assembly in the front view of the lower drawing. With the **Polyline** and **Arc** tools construct a three-view orthographic projection of the spindle assembled in its end brackets. Do not include any dimensions.

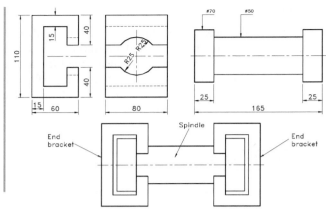

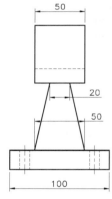

End bracket

Spindle

End bracket

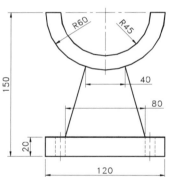

HOLES ⌀10

R20

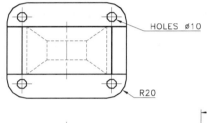

3 A three-view orthographic drawing of a supporting bracket is shown. Construct the three views working to the same procedures used when constructing Example 4 on page 45. Use the tools **Polyline** and **Arc**.

Do not include any dimensions in your drawing.

4 With the tools **Polyline**, **Circle** and **Arc** construct the three views shown here. Do not attempt to include the dimensions.

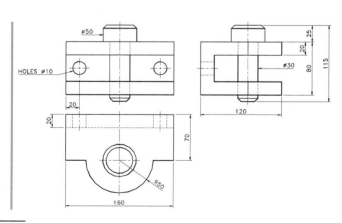

HOLES ⌀10

CHAPTER 7

Other Draw tools

The Polygon tool

The **Polygon** tool can be called either with a *left-click* on its tool icon in the **Draw** toolbar, from its name in the **Draw** pull-down menu, or by entering **pol** at the Command Line. When called, the Command Line shows:

> **Command: _polygon Number of sides <4>:**

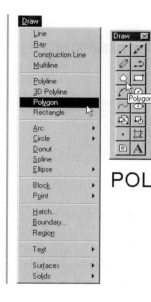

□ **EXAMPLE** □ *various polygons*

Command: _polygon Number of sides <4>: *enter* 6 *right-click*
Edge/<Center of polygon>: *enter* 110,230 *right-click*
Inscribed in circle/Circumscribed about circle[I/C] <I>: *right-click*
Radius of circle: *enter* 60 *right-click*
Command:

POL

Open your drawing template and draw polygons as shown.

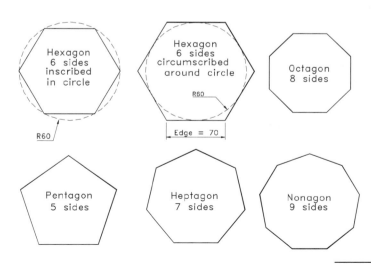

The Ellipse tool

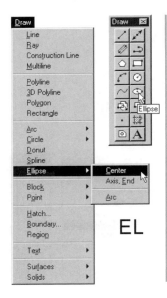

The **Ellipse** tool can be called either with a *left-click* on its tool icon in the **Draw** toolbar, from its name in the **Draw** pull-down menu, or by entering **el** at the Command Line. Note that unlike the **Polygon** tool, when calling **Ellipse** from the **Draw** pull-down menu, a sub-menu appears. When called, the Command Line shows:

> **Command _ellipse**
> **<Axis endpoint 1>/Center:**

☐ **EXAMPLE** ☐ *various ellipses*

Open your drawing template and draw ellipses using the various prompts in the **Ellipse** command sequence.

> **Command: _ellipse**
> **<Axis endpoint 1>/Center:** *enter* c (Center) *right-click*
> **Center of ellipse:** *enter* 140,110 *right-click*
> **Axis endpoint:** *enter* 20,110 *right-click*
> **<Other axis distance>/Rotation:** *enter* 140,140 *right-click*
> **Command:**

☐ **NOTES** ☐

1 The longest axis of an ellipse is its **major axis**. The smaller axis is its **minor axis**.

2 Ellipses in AutoCAD can be constructed as true ellipses or as polylines. The variable **Pellipse** controls which is to be constructed. When **Pellipse** is set to 0 the resulting ellipse will be true. If set to 1, the ellipse will be a polyline. To set **Pellipse**:

> **Command:** *enter* pellipse *right-click*
> **New value for PELLIPSE <0>:** *enter* 1 *right-click*
> **Command:**

3 An ellipse can be regarded as the result of looking at a full circle and then rotating it about its horizontal diameter. As the rotation increases, so the vertical axis becomes shorter and what appears to be an ellipse is seen. The **Rotation** prompt asks the operator to *enter* the angle through which the rotation takes place.

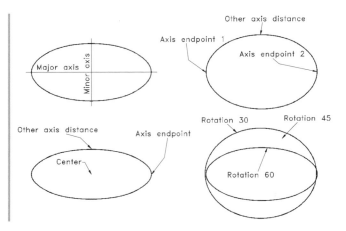

The Rectangle tool

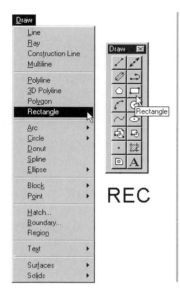

REC

The **Rectangle** tool can be called either with a *left-click* on its tool icon in the **Draw** toolbar, from its name in the **Draw** pull-down menu, or by entering **rec** at the Command Line. When called, the Command Line shows:

Command: _rectang
First corner: either *pick* a point on screen or *enter* coordinate numbers followed by a *right-click*
Other corner: either *pick* a point on screen or *enter* coordinate numbers followed by a *right-click*
Command:

The rectangle then forms on the screen.

□ **NOTE** □
The outline of a rectangle is a polyline, its width depending upon the current **Polyline** setting.

EXERCISES

1   Draw the pentagon (**Polygon** tool). Add its diagonals (**Line** tool). **Erase** the pentagon. Draw the hexagon (**Polygon** tool). Then add its inscribing circle (**Circle** tool). Draw the hexagon again, then add hexagons at each corner with edge lengths of 30. Use the End osnap to accurately position the hexagons at the corners.

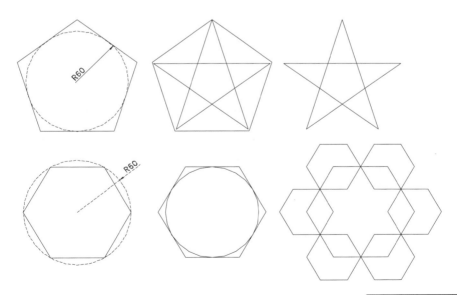

2 With the **Ellipse** tool draw four identical ellipses to form this pattern. Add the inscribing circle at the centre of the pattern using the **Circle** tool.

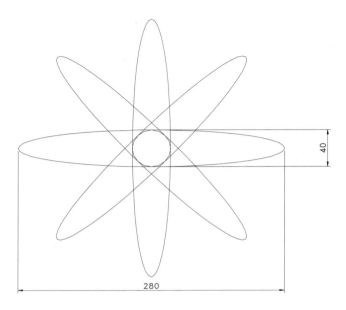

3 With the **Polyline**, **Ellipse** and **Circle** tools, construct the outline of this plate to the given size. Do not include any of the dimensions.

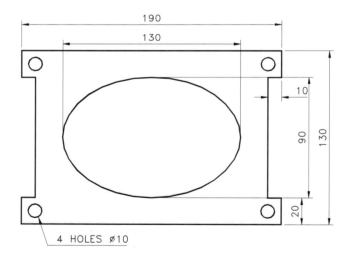

4 HOLES ⌀10

4 With the same tools, construct the outline shown to the given dimensions. Do not include any of the dimensions.

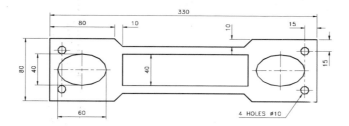

5 With the **Polygon** tool, construct the four given polygons on a common centre. Then add the inscribing circles on the **Hidden** layer. Do not include the dimensions.

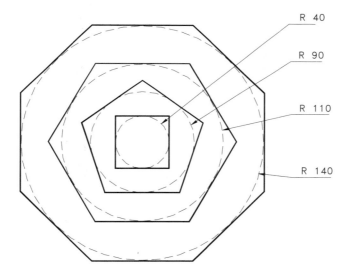

CHAPTER 8
Some Modify tools

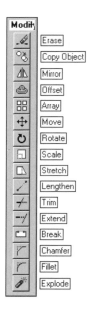

When AutoCAD is opened, the **Modify** toolbox is usually in position **docked** against the **Draw** toolbox on the left-hand side of the window. As the name implies, tools from the **Modify** toolbar are for modifying or editing constructions on screen.

The **Modify** tools **Copy Object**, **Move**, **Trim**, **Array** and **Mirror** will be shown in this chapter. Some other tools from the toolbar will be shown in later chapters.

The **Modify** tools can be called from the toolbar, from the **Modify** pull-down menu, or by *entering* abbreviations for the tools at the Command Line.

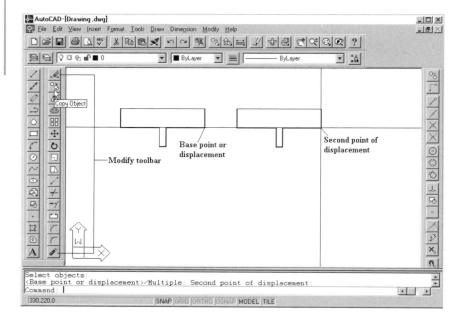

The Copy Object tool

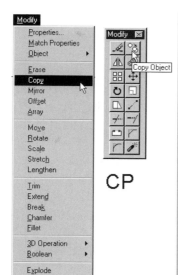

To call the **Copy Object** tool, either *left-click* on its icon in the **Modify** toolbar, or on its name in the **Modify** pull-down menu, or *enter* **cp** at the Command Line.

☐ **EXAMPLE 1** ☐ *single copy*

Open your drawing template and construct the left-hand drawing.

> **Command: _copy**
> **Select objects:** *pick* the keyhole outline (a single pline)
>   **1 found**
> **Select objects:** *right-click*
> **<Base point or displacement>/Multiple:** *pick*
> **Second point of displacement:** *pick*
> **Command:**

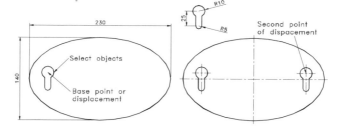

☐ **EXAMPLE 2** ☐ *multiple copies*

Open your drawing template and construct the left-hand drawing.

> **Command: _copy**
> **Select objects:** *enter* w *right-click*
> **First corner:** *pick* **Other corner:** *pick* **2 found**
> **Select objects:** *right-click*
> **<Base point or displacement>/**
>   **Multiple:** *enter* m *right-click*
> **Base point:** *pick* **Second point of**
>   **displacement:** *pick* **Second**
>   **point of displacement:** *pick*
>   **Second point of**
>   **displacement:** *pick* **Second**
>   **point of displacement:** *right-click*
> **Command:**

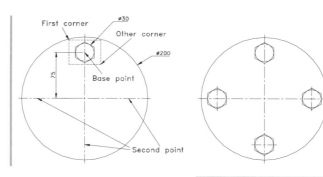

M

The Move tool

To call the **Move** tool, either *left-click* on its icon in the **Modify** toolbar, or on its name in the **Modify** pull-down menu, or *enter* **m** at the Command Line.

☐ **EXAMPLE** ☐

Open your drawing template. Draw the left-hand drawing.

> **Command:** *enter* m *right-click*
> **Select objects:** *enter* w *right-click*
> **First corner:** *pick* **Other corner:** *pick* **2 found**
> **Base point or displacement:** *pick*
> **Second point of displacement:** *pick*
> **Command:**

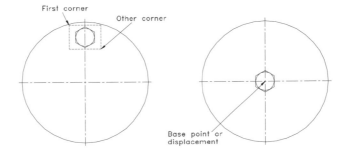

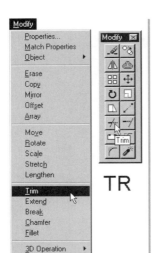

TR

The Trim tool

To call the **Trim** tool, either *left-click* on its icon in the **Modify** toolbar, or on its name in the **Modify** pull-down menu, or *enter* **tr** at the Command Line.

☐ **EXAMPLE 1** ☐

Open your drawing template. Draw the left-hand drawing. Then:

> **Command:** _trim
> **Select cutting edge (Projmode = UCS, Edgemode = No extend)**
> **Select objects:** *right-click* **1 found**
> **Select objects:** *right-click*
> **<Select object to trim>/Project/Edge/Undo:** *pick*
> **<Select object to trim>/Project/Edge/Undo:** *pick*

<Select object to trim>/Project/Edge/Undo: *right-*
click
Command:

□ **EXAMPLE 2** □

Try these other **Trim** operations.

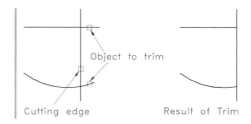

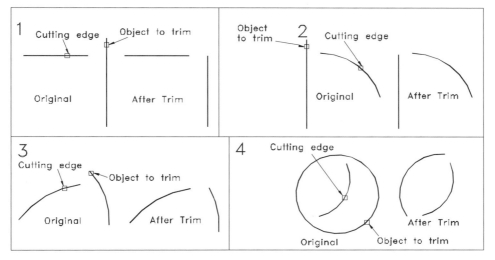

The Mirror tool

MI

To call the **Mirror** tool, either *left-click* on its icon in the
Modify toolbar, or on its name in the **Modify** pull-down
menu, or *enter* **mi** at the Command Line.

□ **EXAMPLE 1** □

Draw the left-hand drawing.

    Command: _mirror
    Select objects: *enter* **w** *right-click*
    First corner: *pick* **Other corner:** *pick* **8 found**
    Select objects: *right-click*
    First point on mirror line: *pick* **Second point:** *pick*
    Delete old objects <N>: *right-click*
    Command:

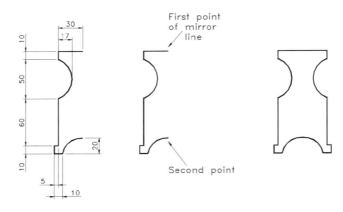

First point
of mirror
line

Second point

☐ **EXAMPLE 2** ☐

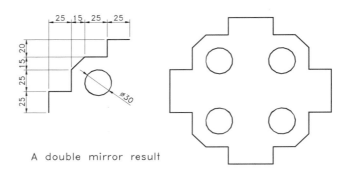

A double mirror result

The Array tool

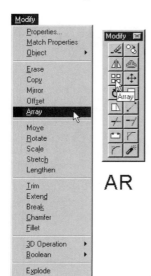

AR

To call the **Array** tool, either *left-click* on its icon in the **Modify** toolbar, or on its name in the **Modify** pull-down menu, or *enter* **ar** at the Command Line.

☐ **EXAMPLE 1** ☐ *rectangular*

Open your template, draw the left-hand drawing.

> **Command:** *enter* ar *right-click*
> **ARRAY**
> **Select objects:** *pick* on corner **Other corner:** *pick* **2 found**
> **Rectangular or Polar array (<R>:/P):** *right-click*
> **Number of rows (---) <1>:** *enter* 4 *right-click*
> **Number of columns (||||) <1>:** *enter* 4 *right-click*
> **Unit cell or distance between rows (---):** *enter* -60 *right-click*
> **Distance between columns (||||):** *enter* 60 *right-click*
> **Command:**

The distance between rows may well be a negative number. This is because the distance between rows is measured along the *y* coordinate axis.

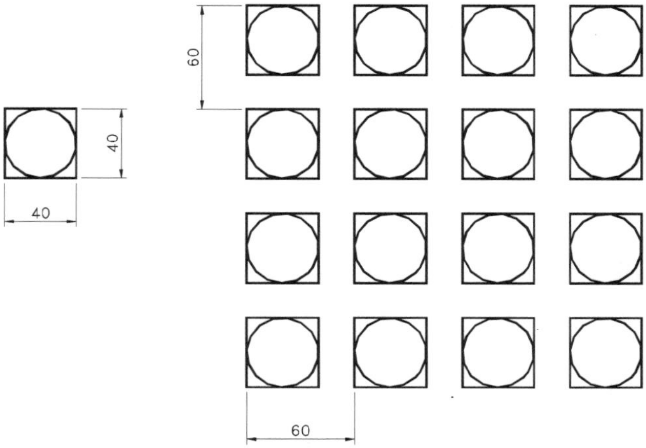

□ **EXAMPLE 2** □ *polar*

Command: array
Select objects: *pick* on corner **Other corner:** *pick* **2 found**
Rectangular or Polar array (<R>:/P): *enter* p *right-click*
Base/<Specify center point of array>: *pick* or *enter* coordinates *right-click*
Number of items: *enter* 8 *right-click*
Angle to fill (+ = ccw, – = cw) <360>: *right-click*
Rotate objects as they are copied <Y>:
Command:

Center point of array

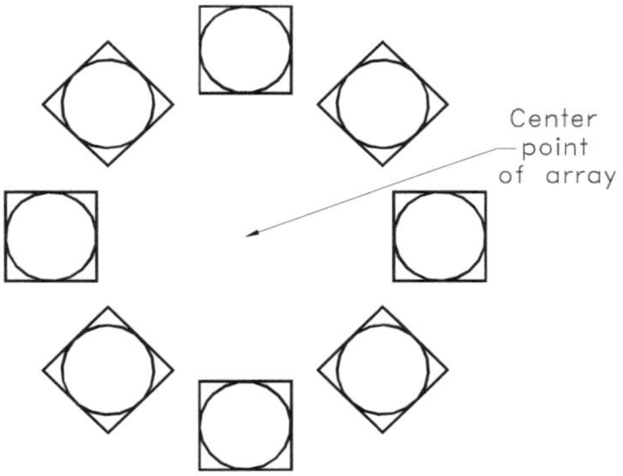

□ **EXAMPLE 3** □ *polar*

Open your template drawing. Construct the circle within a square.

Command: array
Select objects: *pick* on corner **Other corner:** *pick* **2 found**
Rectangular or Polar array (<R>:/P): *enter* p *right-click*
Base/<Specify center point of array>: *pick*
Number of items: *enter* 5 *right-click*
Angle to fill (+ = ccw, – = cw) <360>: *enter* 180 *right-click*
Rotate objects as they are copied <Y>:
Command:

Angle to fill = 180°

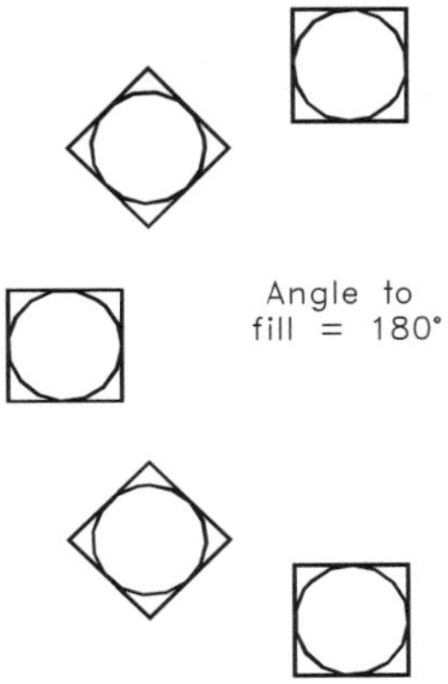

The Offset tool

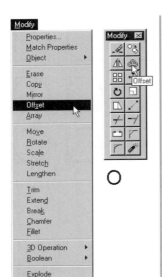

To call the **Offset** tool, either *left-click* on its icon in the **Modify** toolbar, or on its name in the **Modify** pull-down menu, or *enter* **o** at the Command Line. Work the following on your template drawing:

> **Command:** *enter* o *right-click*
> **Offset distance or Through <Through>:** *enter* 10 *right-click*
> **Select object to offset:** *pick* original
> **Side to offset:** *pick* to the side on which the offset is to be
> **Select object to offset:** *right-click*
> **Command:**

☐ **NOTE** ☐

The **Offset distance** can be given by *picking* two points on screen the required offset distance apart.

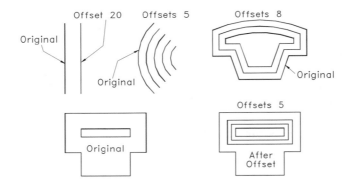

QUESTIONS

1   Which toolbars are usually found **docked** against the left-hand side of the AutoCAD window after start-up?
2   What is the purpose of the **Multiple** prompt of the **Copy Object** Command Line sequence?
3   What is the command abbreviation for the **Offset** tool?
4   When using the **Array** tool for constructing rectangular arrays, why is that, when setting up rows, it is often necessary to *enter* a negative distance between the rows?
5   When using the **Trim** tool have you practised using the **Edge** prompt? If you have, what is its purpose?

These exercises incorporate some revision work based on examples given in previous chapters.

1 Construct the given drawing with the aid of the **Array** tool in **Polar** mode.

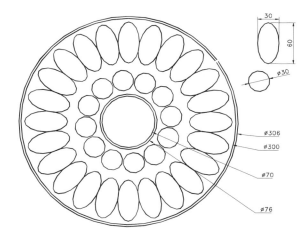

2 Construct the given drawing of a spring clip. You will need to use the **Circle** tool in **TTR** mode, the **Trim** tool and the **Edit Polyline** tool to obtain an accurate outline.

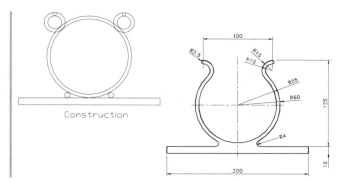

3 Construct the outline of a tool handle to the given dimensions. You will need to use the tools:

Circle in **TTR** mode
Trim
Polyline

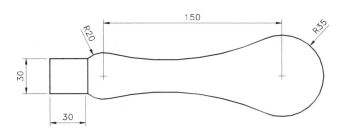

4 With the aid of the tools **Line**, **Polygon**, **Circle**, **Array**, **Trim** and **Edit Polyline** construct the three outlines to the details given.

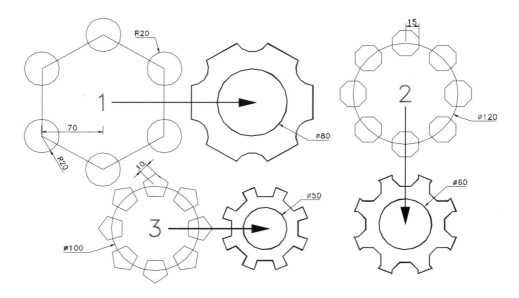

5 Construct this rectangular **Array** to the given sizes. Also try using **Copy** for the same drawing.

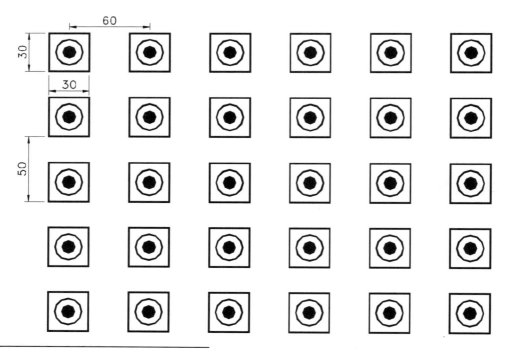

6 Working to any convenient sizes, construct the polar **arrays** as shown.

The left-hand drawing is composed of ellipses, which have been trimmed to the central circle.

The right-hand array is composed of polylines which have been constructed to varying widths.

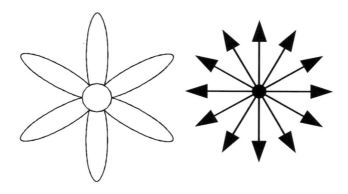

7 Construct the outline with the aid of the **Polyline** tool to a **Width** of **0.7**. Then offset to the **Offset distances** as shown.

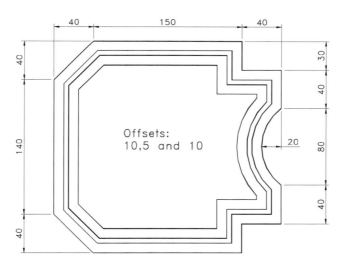

CHAPTER 9

More Modify tools

The Break tool

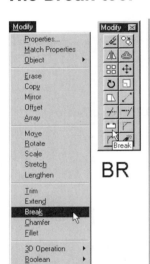

BR

To call the **Break** tool, either *left-click* on its icon in the **Modify** toolbar, or on its name in the **Modify** pull-down menu, or *enter* **br** at the Command Line.

☐ **EXAMPLE 1** ☐ *a line, an arc and a circle*

Open your drawing template.

> **Command:** *enter br right-click*
> **BREAK Select object:** *pick*
> **Enter second point (or F for first point):** *pick*
> **Command:**

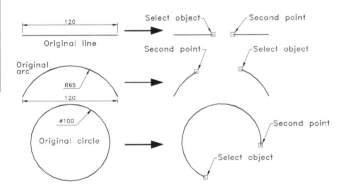

☐ **EXAMPLE 2** ☐ *using the First option*

Open your drawing template and copy the arc and circle (left-hand drawings).

> **Command:** *enter br right-click*
> **BREAK Select object:** *pick*
> **Enter second point (or F for first point):** *enter f right-click*
> **Enter first point:** *pick*
> **Enter second point:** *pick*
> **Command:**

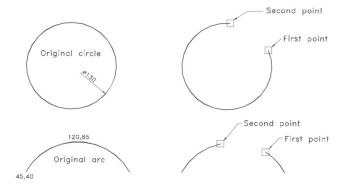

Original circle

Ø130

Second point

First point

120,85

Original arc

45,40

Second point

First point

The Scale tool

SC

To call the **Scale** tool, either *left-click* on its icon in the **Modify** toolbar, or on its name in the **Modify** pull-down menu, or *enter* **sc** at the Command Line.

□ **EXAMPLE** □

Open your template drawing. Then draw the original and use the **Multiple Copy** to copy it five times. Then:

> **Command:** _scale
> **Select objects:** *pick* first copy
> **Select objects:** *right-click*
> **Base point:** *pick*
> **<Scale factor>/Reference:** *enter* 0.5 *right-click*
> **Command:**

Continue for the other four copies, scaling to the figures shown in the drawings.

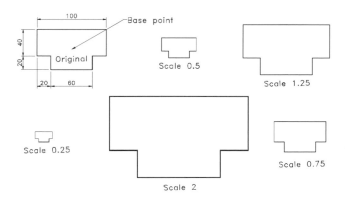

100

40

20

Base point

Original

20   60

Scale 0.5

Scale 1.25

Scale 0.25

Scale 0.75

Scale 2

The Stretch tool

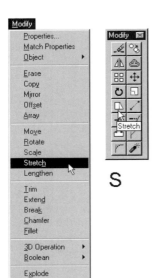

To call the **Stretch** tool, either *left-click* on its icon in the **Modify** toolbar, or on its name in the **Modify** pull-down menu, or *enter* **s** at the Command Line.

Open your drawing template. Construct the top-left drawing and copy it to the lower drawing.

Command: _stretch
Select objects by crossing-window or crossing-polygon
Select objects: *enter* c *right-click*
First corner: *pick* **Second corner:** *pick*
Base point or displacement: *pick*
Second point of displacement: *pick*
Command:

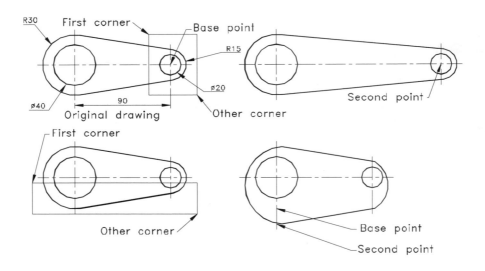

□ **NOTE** □

If an attempt is made to **Stretch** a circle, the attempt will fail, but arcs can be acted upon by the tool

---

The Rotate tool

RO

To call the **Rotate** tool, either *left-click* on its icon in the **Modify** toolbar, or on its name in the **Modify** pull-down menu, or *enter* **ro** at the Command Line.

Open your drawing template. Construct the arrow and circle shown in the top-left drawing. Multiple **Copy** the drawing six times.

Command: *enter* ro *right-click*
Select objects: *window the objects* **2 found**
Select objects: *right-click*
Base point: *pick*
<Rotation angle>/Reference: *enter* 30 *right-click*
Command:

Continue in this manner for each of the other five arrows, rotating to the figures as shown.

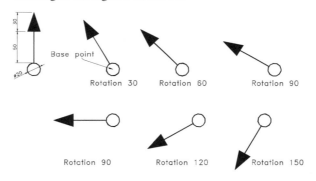

The Extend tool

EX

To call the **Extend** tool, either *left-click* on its icon in the **Modify** toolbar, or on its name in the **Modify** pull-down menu, or *enter* **ex** at the Command Line.

Open your drawing template. Copy the three drawings and practise using the **Extend** tool on the objects as shown.

Command: _extend
Select boundary edges: (Projmode = UCS, Edgemode = No extend)
Select objects: *pick* **1 found**
Select objects: *right-click*
<Select object to extend>/Project/Edge/Undo: *pick*
<Select object to extend>/Project/Edge/Undo: *right-click*
Command:

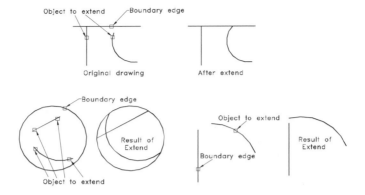

QUESTIONS

1 When using the **Break** tool, what purpose is served by the **F** response?
2 When using the **Break** tool in which direction should breaking occur around a circle?
3 Have you tried using the **Reference** prompt of the **Scale** tool?
4 What happens when **Stretch** is used on a circle?
5 In which direction would you expect a vertical line to rotate when the **Rotate** tool is used to rotate the line by 225°: South East, South West, North West or North East?
6 When using the **Extend** tool what happens when the **Edge** prompt is used in response to the sequence line **<Select object to extend>/Project/Edge/Undo:**?
7 What are the abbreviations for the tools **Break**, **Scale**, **Stretch** and **Extend**?

□ WORKED EXAMPLE 1 □

1 Open your drawing template.
2 **Snap** should be on and set to 5 in your drawing template. If it is not so set:

Command: *enter* snap *right-click*
Snap spacing or ON/OFF/Aspect/Rotate/
   Style <10>: *enter* 5 *right-click*
Command:

The **SNAP** indicator in the status bar should show black. If it doesn't, *double-click* to set **SNAP** on.

3 **Stage 1**: Construct the circles and polyline to the details given.
4 **Stage 2**: With the aid of the **Trim** tool, trim the polyline and the Ø30 circle back to the Ø140 circle.

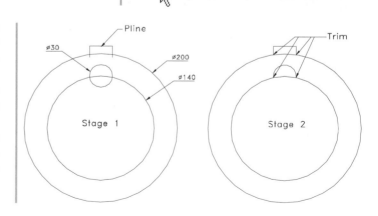

5 **Stage 3**: With the **Array** tool, polar array the polyline 12 times around the Ø200 circle.

6 With the **Rotate** tool, rotate the part circle 60°.

7 With the aid of the **Mirror** tool, mirror the part circle to the right, then mirror both part circles vertically downwards.

8 **Stage 4**: With the **Trim** tool, trim away parts of the circles no longer required.

9 **Stage 5**: With the aid of the **Edit Polyline** tool, convert the two parts of the finished drawing into single polylines by using the **Join** command. (This may require using a window.)

10 **Final drawing**: With the aid of the **Edit Polyline** tool change the line width to 1.

11 Set the layer **Centre** as the current layer and add centre lines as shown.

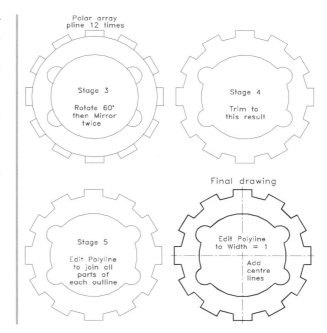

□ **WORKED EXAMPLE 2** □

1 Open your drawing template.

2 Construct the left-hand drawing, taking particular note of the two centre lines at angles of 15° to vertical. Use the Int osnap to ensure that the R7.5 circles are accurately positioned.

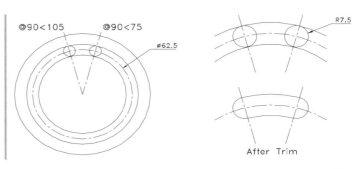

3 With the aid of the **Trim** tool trim the circles as shown in the right-hand drawing.

4 Use the **Edit Polyline** tool to join the arcs and then change their line width of the trimmed arcs to 0.7.

5 With the polar setting of **Array** repeat the group of arcs six times around the centre of the Ø170 circle.

6 Add the circle Ø50.

7 Change the line widths of the circles to 0.7. This involves the use of the **Break** tool and the **Edit Polyline** tool.

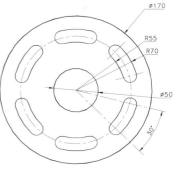

1   Working to the construction details as shown, construct the right-hand drawing. Use the tools **Circle**, **Line**, **Array**, **Trim** and **Edit Polyline**.

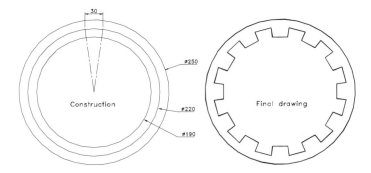

2   Working to the details given in the left-hand drawing, construct the right-hand drawing. Use the tools **Circle**, **Line**, **Array**, **Trim** and **Edit Polyline**.

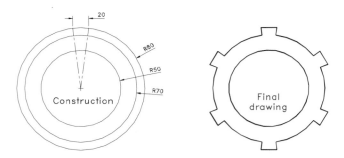

3   Construct the left-hand drawing to the given sizes. Multiple **Copy** the drawing twice, followed by rotating each to the angles shown using the **Rotate** tool.

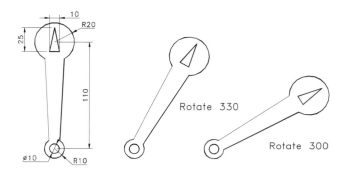

4 Construct the left-hand drawing to the dimensions given with the aid of the **Polyline**, **Circle** and **Trim** tools. Multiple **Copy** the drawing twice. Using the **Scale** tool reduce the copies to the scales shown.

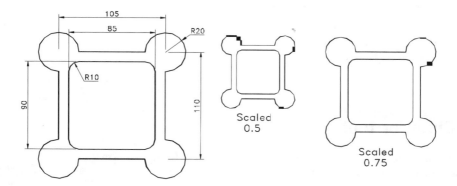

5 Working to the construction and sizes shown in the left-hand drawing, construct the right-hand drawing. Use the tools **Circle**, **Line**, **Array**, **Trim** and **Edit Polyline**.

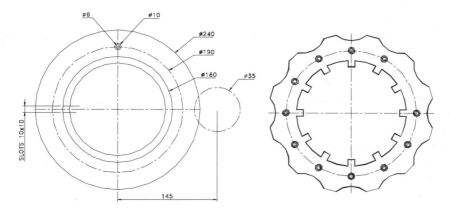

CHAPTER 10

Chamfer and Fillet

The Chamfer tool

Chamfer can be called from the **Modify** toolbar, from the **Modify** pull-down menu, or by *entering* **cha** at the Command Line.

□ **EXAMPLE 1** □

Open your drawing template. Construct a rectangle with the aid of the **Line** tool. Call **Chamfer**. The Command Line shows:

> **Command: _chamfer**
> **(TRIM mode) Current chamfer Dist1 = 10, Dist2 = 10**
> **Polyline/Distance/Angle/Trim/Method/<Select first line>:**
>   *enter* d *right-click*
> **Enter first chamfer distance <10>:** *enter* 15 *right-click*
> **Enter second chamfer distance <15>:** *right-click*
> **Command:** *right-click*
> **(TRIM mode) Current chamfer Dist1 = 15, Dist2 = 15**
> **Polyline/Distance/Angle/Trim/Method/<Select first line>:**
>   *pick* top line
> **Select second line:** *pick* right-hand line
> **Command:**

Then repeat for top and left-hand lines.

□ **EXAMPLE 2** □

Construct a rectangle with the aid of the **Polyline** tool. Call **Chamfer**. The Command Line shows:

> **Command: _chamfer**
> **(TRIM mode) Current chamfer Dist1 = 15, Dist2 = 15**
> **Polyline/Distance/Angle/Trim/Method/<Select first line>:** *enter* p *right-click*
> **Select 2D polyline:** *pick*
> **4 lines were chamfered**
> **Command:**

Construct any two lines which do not meet. Set **Dist1** and **Dist2** to 0 and the lines are extended to meet when the **Chamfer** tool is used. If the lines had crossed, or one had extended beyond the other, the result would have been the same – the lines would form a corner join.

□ **EXAMPLE 4** □

No matter how complicated a closed polyline is, when chamfering with the **Polyline** prompt, all corners become chamfered.

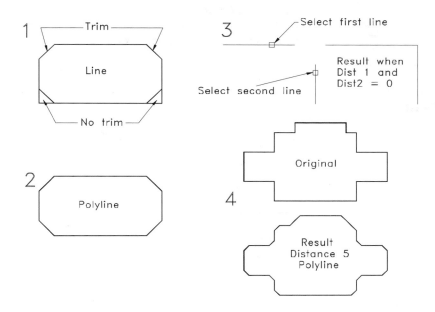

□ **NOTES** □

1 If a chamfer is to be constructed, with the distance along the first line different to that along the second line, the response to the following prompt should be **a** (Angle):

Polyline/Distance/Angle/Trim/Method/<Select first line>: *enter* t *right-click*

The two distances can then be different.

2 If the edges in drawing 1 are not to be trimmed, the response to the prompt should be **t** (Trim):

Polyline/Distance/Angle/Trim/Method/<Select first line>:

In this case another prompt appears:

Trim/No trim/<Trim>: *enter* n (No trim) *right-click*

The Fillet tool

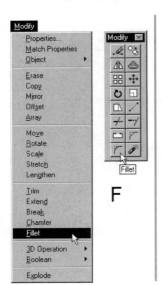

Fillet can be called from the **Modify** toolbar, from the **Modify** pull-down menu, or by *entering* **f** at the Command Line.

□ **EXAMPLE 1** □

Prompts for **Fillet** are similar to **Chamfer**, but instead of settings figures for distances (**Dist1** and **Dist2**) the operator sets figures for **Radius**.

The four examples shown were constructed using similar responses as those for the **Chamfer** examples.

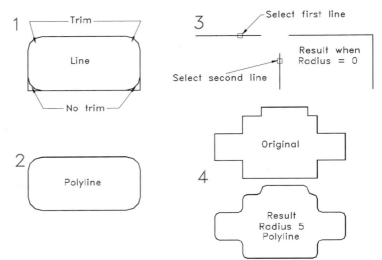

□ **EXAMPLE 2** □ *fillets between lines and circles*

It is possible to fillet between circles or arcs, between circles and lines, or between arcs. Two examples are given – the first (drawing 1) between a circle and a line, the second (drawing 2) between circles.

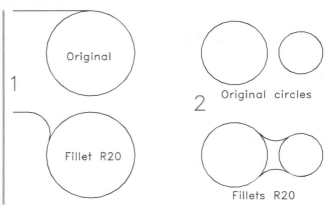

1 Is it possible to fillet one corner of a polyline rectangle?
2 Is it possible to use the **Fillet** tool to form a sharp corner from two lines which do not meet at the corner?
3 What is the abbreviation for the **Chamfer** tool?
4 What is the abbreviation for the **Fillet** tool?
5 Can a fillet be formed between two adjacent circles?

EXERCISES

1 Construct the outline on the right with the aid of the **Polyline**, **Fillet** and **Chamfer** tools. Do not attempt to include any of the dimensions.
2 Construct the ratchet wheel outline shown below. Use the tools **Line**, **Circle**, **Array** (polar), **Fillet** and **Edit Polyline**.

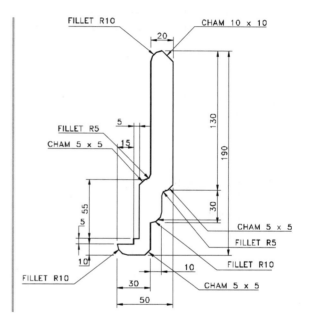

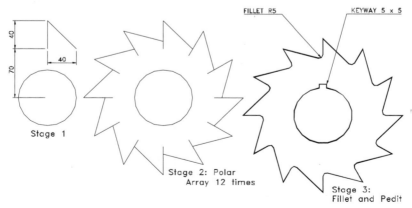

3 Construct a three-view orthographic drawing of the angle bracket shown.

Your views should show two bolts positioned in the holes of the base of the bracket, with the washers and nuts in a suitable position.

Use the tools **Polyline** (or **Line**), **Circle** and **Chamfer**. You may wish to use **Edit Polyline** if you have used the **Line** tool.

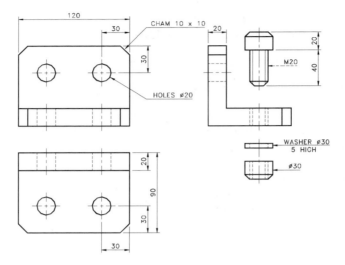

4 Construct the outline of the fitting shown. You will find it easiest to start using the **Line** and **Circle** tools, followed by using **Trim** and the **Fillet** tool, before using **Edit Polyline** to finish with a line width of say 0.5.

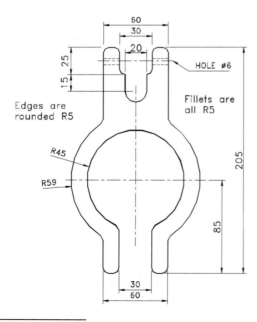

5 A two-view drawing of a pulley wheel is shown. Working to the dimensions given, construct the two views. Do not include any of the dimensions.

Use the **Circle**, **Polyline** (or **Line**), **Array** and **Fillet** tools. You may also wish to use **Edit Polyline**.

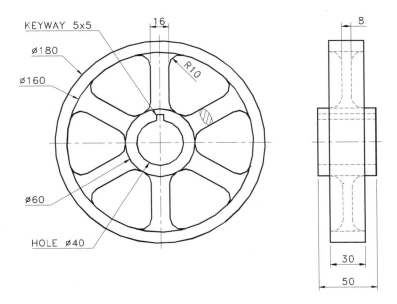

6 Working to the dimensions given, construct the outline of the plate shown. Do not include any of the dimensions. Start by constructing the outline with the **Line** tool, followed by the **Fillet** and **Chamfer** tools.

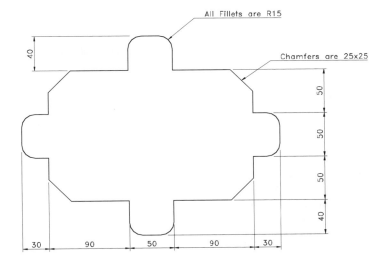

CHAPTER 11

Hatching

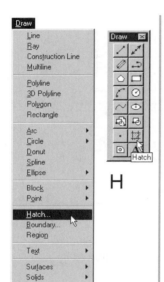

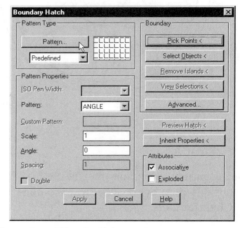

To call the **Hatch** tool, either *left-click* on the **Hatch** icon in the **Draw** toolbar or on **Hatch...** in the **Draw** pull-down menu, or *enter* **h** at the Command Line.

Any one of these calls brings the **Boundary Hatch** dialogue box on screen.

☐ **EXAMPLE 1** ☐ *hatching an area*

1 Open your drawing template and draw a polyline of size 200 by 140.

2 Call the **Hatch** tool. The **Boundary Hatch** dialogue box appears.

3 *Left-click* on the **Pattern** button to bring up the first of three **Hatch pattern palettes**. More patterns can be seen by *clicking* the **Next** button.

4 *Left-click* in required pattern: **ANSI31**. *Left-click* on the **OK** button. The **Boundary Hatch** dialogue box reappears; **ANSI31** appears in the **Pattern** box of the dialogue box.

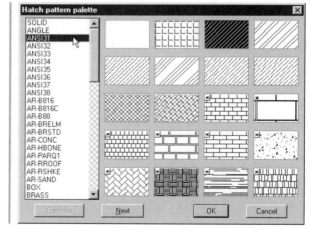

5 *Enter* **2** in the **Scale** box of the dialogue box.

6 *Left-click* on the **Pick Points <** button. The dialogue box disappears. *Left-click* within the rectangle to be hatched. The rectangle highlights as a broken line. *Right-click* to return to the **Boundary Hatch** dialogue box.

7 *Left-click* on the **Preview Hatch** button of the dialogue box. The rectangle is hatched with the **ANSI31** pattern. A message box appears with a **Continue** button in its centre.

8 *Left-click* on the **Continue** button, which brings back the dialogue box. If the hatching is as desired, *left-click* on the **Apply** button of the dialogue box and the rectangle is hatched.

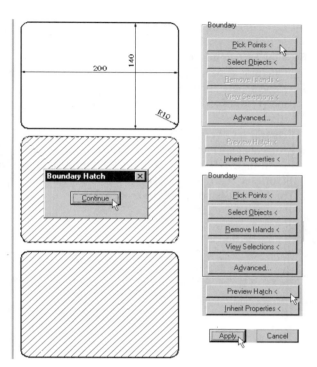

□ **NOTE** □

1 If the preview of the hatching does not show the desired result, changes made in the pattern, scale or angle will appear when the **Preview Hatch <** button is used again.

2 When selecting an area to be hatched, it must be a closed boundary. If an area is picked which is not closed – even with only the slightest gap in the outline – the **Boundary Definition Error** box will appear. This does not necessarily mean the area cannot be hatched. Try the **Select Objects <** button and instead *pick* each object forming the boundary of the area to be hatched.

□ **EXAMPLE 2** □ *advanced options*

1 Draw three sets of concentric circles (diameters 110, 90, 70, 50 and 30).

2 *Left-click* on the **Pattern** button and select the pattern **SOLID** from the first **Hatch pattern palette**.

3 In the **Boundary Hatch** dialogue box *left-click* on the **Advanced...** button. The **Advanced Options** dialogue box comes on screen.

4 In the **Style** popup list set the **Style** to **Normal**, followed by a *left-click* on the **OK** button. The **Boundary Hatch** dialogue box reappears.

5 *Left-click* on the **Select Objects <** button and *left-click* on each circle of the left-hand set.

6 The left-hand set of circles now show hatching as below.

7 Repeat, but with the **Outer** name *picked* from the **Style** popup list of the **Advanced Options** dialogue box. The result is shown in the central set of circles below.

8 Repeat again after selecting the **Ignore** name from the **Style** popup list of the **Advanced Options** dialogue box. The result is shown in the right-hand set of circles below.

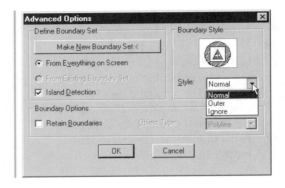

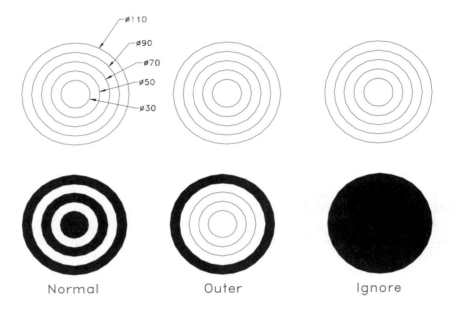

| Normal | Outer | Ignore |

☐ **EXAMPLE 3** ☐ *associative hatching*

1 Open your drawing template and construct the left-hand drawing on page 81. The hatching is **BRICK** with **Scale** set to 1.

2 When a boundary inside a hatched area is moved the hatching accommodates the shift. This is known as 'associative hatching'.

3 Call **Move**. Window the rectangle; it can be *dragged* to another position within or even outside the hatched area. See the right-hand drawing.

☐ **NOTE** ☐

For associative hatching to function correctly, the **Associative** check box must be set 'on' (tick in box) in the **Attributes** area of the **Boundary Hatch** dialogue box.

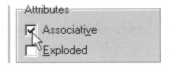

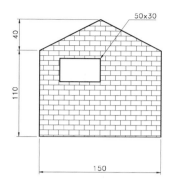
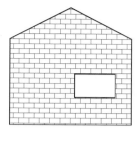

□ **EXAMPLE 4** □ *a sectional view in an engineering drawing*

A two-view third angle projection of an attachment bracket is shown. The sectional view (left-hand view) is obtained by imagining a vertical plane cutting through the pin and its bracket, its edge signified by the **A** labels with arrows (right-hand view) pointing in the direction from which the sectional view is to be obtained. The section plane is imagined as cutting through the parts of the assembly; what is in front of the view as seen from the right is thrown away, leaving a view of the cut surface.

The cut surface is then hatched. It is customary to use the ANSI31 hatch pattern for this purpose in engineering drawings – lines at angle of 45° with **Scale** set to 2. This example shows some of the rules governing section hatching:

1 The edge of the section plane is shown as a centre line ending in thick lines with arrows pointing in the direction from which the sectional view should be seen.
2 The sectional view is labelled with the letters on the section plane line.
3 The arrows on the section plane line carry letters labelling the sectional view.
4 Features such as bolts, nuts, screws, ribs, webs and similar parts are shown in section as outside views – thus the pin and web in the example are not hatched, that is, they are shown as outside views.

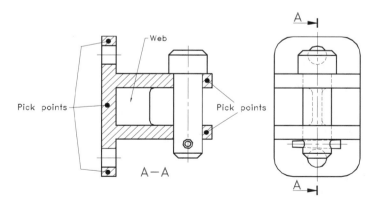

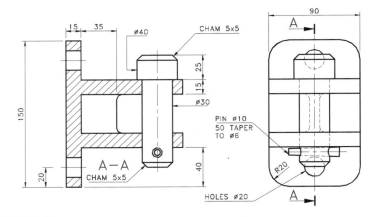

QUESTIONS

1 What is the abbreviation for the **Hatch** tool?
2 What happens if the word **hatch** is *entered* at the Command Line?
3 What is meant by **associative hatching**?
4 How is **associative hatching** set?
5 Can you write down the stages needed to hatch a simple rectangular outline?
6 What happens if a gap appears in an outline about to be hatched?
7 If a gap does appear in an outline to be hatched, what steps can be taken to hatch the area?
8 If the **preview** of a hatched area is not as wished, what steps can be taken to correct the hatch?
9 What is the purpose of the hatching **Advanced Options** dialogue box?
10 What is the hatch pattern commonly used when hatching a **section** in an engineering drawing?

EXERCISES

1 Construct a rectangle to the given dimensions. Multiple **Copy** the rectangle to obtain four rectangles as shown. **Fillet** the corners of the top-left rectangle; **Chamfer** those of the right-top rectangle; cut the corners as shown in the bottom-left rectangle; radius the corners of the bottom-right rectangle.

    Hatch the rectangles following the information given in the drawing.

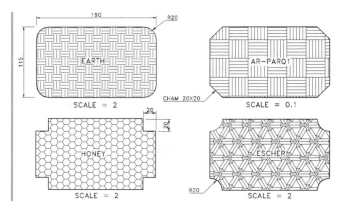

2 With **Polyline**, construct a rectangle, square and circle as shown in the left-hand drawing. Hatch the three outlines to the information given. Make sure associative hatching is set 'on' and then change the positions of the square and circle within the outer rectangle.

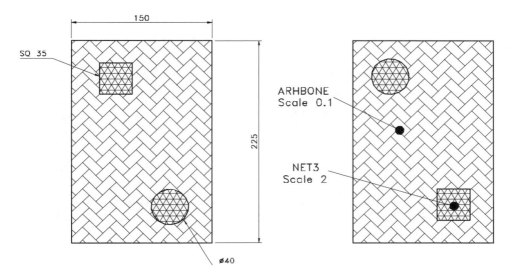

3 When text is placed within an area to be hatched it automatically sets up its own invisible surround, protecting it, as it were, from becoming covered in the hatch pattern. See Chapter 12 concerning the placing of text in a drawing. Then attempt to construct the drawing using any hatch pattern thought to be suitable.

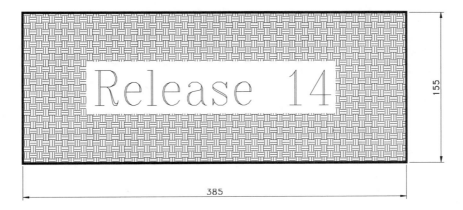

4 Using the **Polyline**, **Hatch** and **Mirror** tools construct the pattern shown.

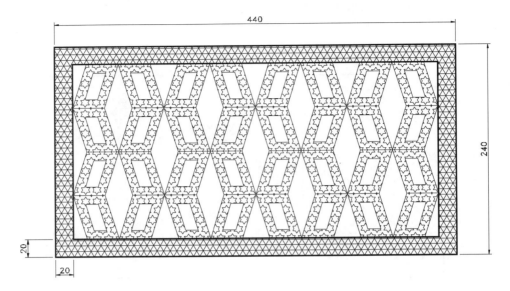

5 Construct a two-view orthographic projection of the faceplate shown below. Use the **Polyline** (or **Line**), **Circle**, **Array** and **Hatch** tools.

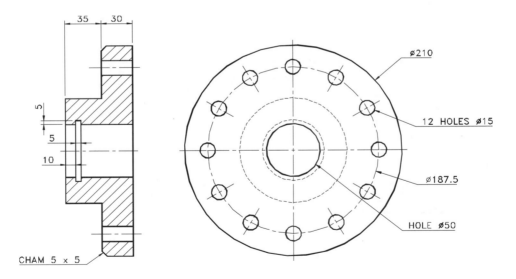

CHAPTER 12

Text

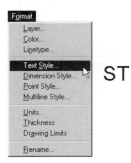

The Text Style dialogue box

Before being able to place any text it is advisable to set the **Text Style** you wish to use first. AutoCAD has numerous text styles. These are set from the **Text Style** dialogue box, called to screen either from the **Format** pull-down menu or by *entering* **st** at the Command Line.

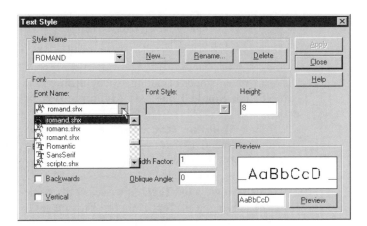

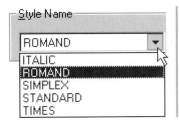

Left-click on the arrow at the side of the **Font Name:** box in the dialogue box. The required text style can be selected from the popup list.

Scrolling this list will eventually show the operator all the text styles available.

Arial
BankGothic Lt BT
BankGothic Md BT
CityBlueprint
Comic Sans MS
CommercialPi BT
CommercialScript BT
Complex
CountryBlueprint
Courier New
Dutch801 Rm BT
Dutch801 XBd BT
EuroRoman
GDT
GothicE
GothicG
GothicI
GreekC
GreekS
ISOCP
ISOCP2
ISOCP3
ISOCT
ISOCT2
ISOCT3
Italic
ItalicC
ItalicT
LotusLineDraw
LotusWPSet
SansSerif
ScriptC
ScriptS
Simplex
Stylus BT
SuperFrench
Swis721 BdCnOul BT
Swis721 BdOul BT
Swis721 Blk BT
Swis721 BlkCn BT
Swis721 BlkOul BT
Swis721 BT
Swis721 Cn BT
Swis721 Ex BT
Swis721 Lt BT
Swis721 LtCn BT
Swis721 LtEx BT
Syastro
Symap
Symath
Symath
Symbol
Symeteo
Symusic
Technic
TechnicBold
TechnicLite
Times New Roman
Txt
UniversalMath1 BT

Left-click on the arrow to the right of the **Style Name:** box and a popup list shows the text styles already loaded.

A new text style can be loaded with a *left-click* on the **New...** button in the **Text Style** dialogue box, followed by selection of a font from the **Font Name:** popup list. The name **Style1** (or similar) which appears can be changed to whatever you wish, such as the name of the selected font style.

□ **NOTES** □

In the **Text Style** dialogue box:

1 The selected font shows in the **Preview** box.
2 The **Height** of the selected font can be set in the **Height** box.
3 The **Width** and **Obliquing Angle** of the selected font can be changed in their respective boxes.
4 Other changes can be made in the **Effects** area of the dialogue box.

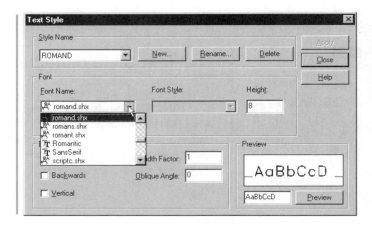

The Text tools

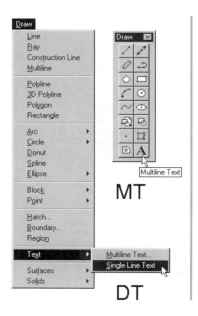

There are two methods of calling text: **Multiline Text** (**mtext**) and **Single Line Text** (**dynamic text** or **dtext**).

To call **Multiline Text**, either select the name from the sub-menu of **Text** from the **Draw** pull-down menu, *pick* its icon from the **Draw** toolbar, or *enter* **mt** at the Command Line.

To call **Single Line Text**, either select the name from the sub-menu of **Text** from the **Format** pull-down menu, or *enter* **dt** at the Command Line.

■ **Multiline text**

1 Call **Mtext**.
2 **Command: _mtext Current text style ROMAND.**
   Text height : 8
   Specify first corner: *pick* or *enter* coordinates
   Specify opposite corner or [Height/Justify/
   Rotate/Style/Width]: *pick* or *enter* coordinates

The **Multiline Text Editor** appears on screen. *Enter* text to be added to the drawing in the **Multiline Text Editor**.

3 *Left-click* on the **OK** button.

4 The text appears in the AutoCAD window in the position of the window chosen when **Mtext** was called.

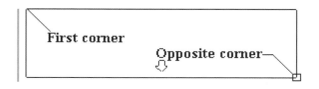

□ **NOTES** □

1 In the **Mutliline Text Editor** another text style other than that currently loaded can be selected from the popup list.

This is the text which will be entered on the screen within the window picked when Mtext is called.

2 If **degrees** (°), the **plus/minus** (±) sign or **diameter** (Ø) are to be included, these can be selected from the **Symbol** menu. If other symbols are required *left-click* on **Other…** in the **Symbol** menu and the Windows **Character Map** appears from which any other symbol can be selected.

3 Experiment with the **Properties** and **Find/Select** tabs in the **Multiline Text Editor**.

■ Single line text

Either select **Single Line Text** from the **Text** sub-menu of the **Draw** pull-down menu, or *enter* **dt** at the Command Line:

> **Command: _dtext Justify/Style/<Start point>:** *pick or enter coordinates*
> **Rotation angle <0>:** *right-click*
> **Text:** *enter required text.*

The text appears at the *picked* position as it is *entered* at the Command Line.

□ **NOTES** □

1 It is advisable to experiment with the **Justify** prompt. This allows text to be *entered* in a variety of positions relating to the point *picked* in response to **Start point:**.

2 When using the **Dtext** method of adding text to a drawing, symbols can be included by *entering* the following:

> **%%d** – Degree symbol: Thus **45%%d** will place 45°.
> **%%c** – Diameter symbol: Thus **%%c45** will place Ø45.

%%p – Tolerance symbol: Thus **45%%p0.5** will place 45±0.5.

%%% – Per cent sign: Thus **45%%%** will place 45%

%%u – Underscore: Thus **%%u45** will place 45.

■ Text styles – some examples

This is Romand text of height 10

This is italic text of height 8

Romans text of height 12

This is Romantic text of height 8

This is Sans Serif text of height 10

This is Simplex text of height 10

Standard (txt.shx) of height 12

This is Times New Roman text of height 10

Times New Romand – width 1.5, oblique 10

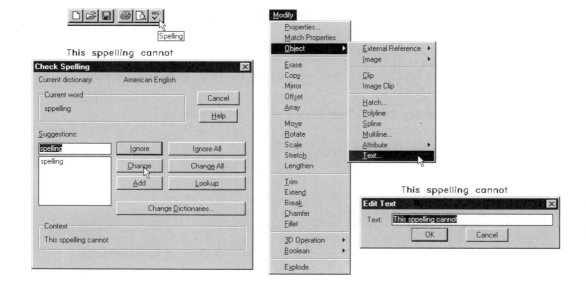

■ Checking spelling

There are two methods of checking spelling in AutoCAD. The first is to use the **Spelling** tool from the **Standard** toolbar, the second is to select **Text...** from **Objects** in the **Modify** pull-down menu. These are shown below. It is advisable to experiment with using these two spelling checkers.

1 Can you name the two types of tools used for placing text in drawings?
2 What is the difference between these two methods of placing text?
3 How can figures including decimals be placed in text in R14?
4 What would you *enter* to show the diameter Ø50 in text in a drawing?
5 How would you *enter* ±0.5 to show in text in a drawing?
6 Can you write down the stages needed to change the text font in use from **ROMAND** to **Times New Roman**?
7 Have you experimented with the **B**old, **I**talic and **U**nderline buttons in the **Multiline Text Editor** dialogue box? They can only be used with Windows True Type Fonts.

EXERCISES

1 Open your drawing template and construct drawing as follows:

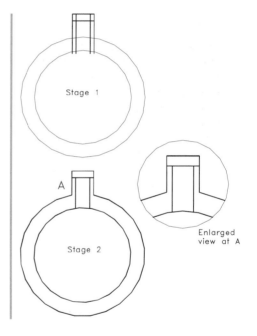

Stage 1

A

Enlarged view at A

Stage 2

Circle – centre 230,120; radius 90.
Circle – centre 230,120; radius 70.
Pline from 230,185 to 230,285.
Offset pline both sides through 10.25.
Offset pline both sides through 15.75.
Erase central pline.
Pline joining tops of outer plines – use End osnap.
Zoom window area of plines.
Trim as shown.
Polyline Edit circles to width 0.7.
Mtext in **Multiline Text Editor** *enter* text as shown – use the **Symbol** pull-down menu. Press **OK** to place text.
Line from text to drawing.

The final drawing should look like the drawing shown on the next page.

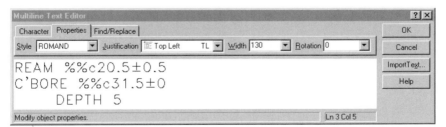

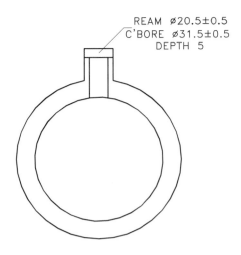

REAM ⌀20.5±0.5
C'BORE ⌀31.5±0.5
DEPTH 5

2 Open your drawing template:

Circle – centre 260,150, radius 120.
Line from centre of circle @120<90.
Line from centre of circle @120<0.
Line from centre of circle @120<280.
Line from centre of circle @120<240.
Line from centre of circle @120<210.
Line from centre of circle @120<175.
Line from centre of circle @120<150.
Line from centre of circle @120<130.
Line from centre of circle @120<109.
Style set to **ROMAND** of **Height** 8.
Dtext – add text around circle as shown using **%%%** for the per cent sign.
Dtext – add text inside circle using the **Rotation angle** prompt to set the angle of the text.
Use **Rotate** and **Move** to rearrange the text inside the circle if necessary.

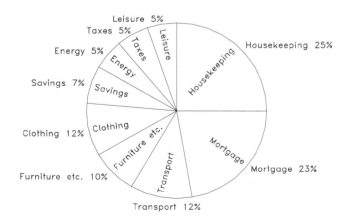

CHAPTER 13

Types of drawing

Orthographic projection

Orthographic projections are the most common form of working technical drawings in the engineering and building industries. In general there are two forms of this type of projection: **first angle** projection and **third angle** projection. In the USA, third angle orthographic projection is that most commonly used, but elsewhere in the world, both angles of projection will be found in about equal proportions.

You will have drawn a number of orthographic projections already if you have been working through the examples and exercises contained in earlier chapters of this book.

Orthographic projections consist of views of the article drawn from a variety of directions, ignoring perspective. Usually three views suffice to describe the article being drawn, but many orthographic projections consist of one, two, three or more views, designed to describe the article as fully as possible. An article consisting of a shaped flat plate may only require one view, more complicated articles may require many. Depending upon the direction from which the article is viewed, the views are named:

- **Front view** – view from the side chosen as the front of the article.
- **End view** – a view from the side of the article.
- **Plan** – usually a view from above, but can also be a view from underneath.

☐ **EXAMPLE 1** ☐ *a third angle projection*

The given views are in third angle projection, with the **plan** (as viewed from above) above the **front view** and **end view**, as viewed looking from the side on which the end view is placed.

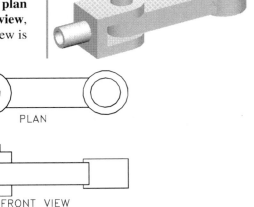

□ **NOTES** □

1 There was really no need for an end view in this example – in the working drawing, the end view was not included.

2 In working drawings (shown right), centre lines, hidden detail lines and dimensions will be added to the views.

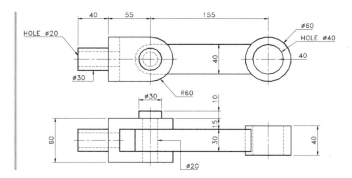

□ **EXAMPLE 2** □ *a first angle projection*

In a first angle orthographic projection, the **plan** (as viewed from above) is placed below the front view, and the **end view** is placed on the **opposite** side to the direction from which the view is seen.

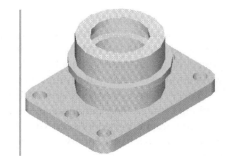

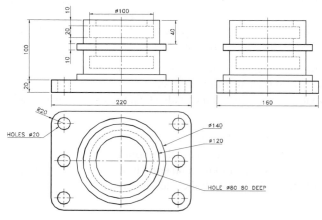

Isometric drawing

The **Grid** and **Snap** settings for constructing isometric drawings are best set in the **Drawing Aids** dialogue box:

■ **Snap** is 'on', **Grid** is 'on' (ticks in the check boxes).
■ **Y Spacing** for **Snap** (5) and **Grid** (10) have been *entered*.

- **Isometric Snap/Grid** is 'on'.
- **Left** isoplane is current.

AutoCAD recognises three isoplanes: **Left**, **Top** and **Right**. The easiest method of setting the required isoplane is to press the **Ctrl** and **E** keys. Repeated pressing of **E** while holding down **Ctrl** toggles between the three isoplanes.

When **Isometric Snap/Grid** is set as in this **Drawing Aids** dialogue box, the AutoCAD window shows as below.

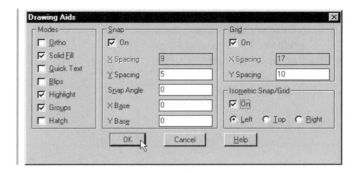

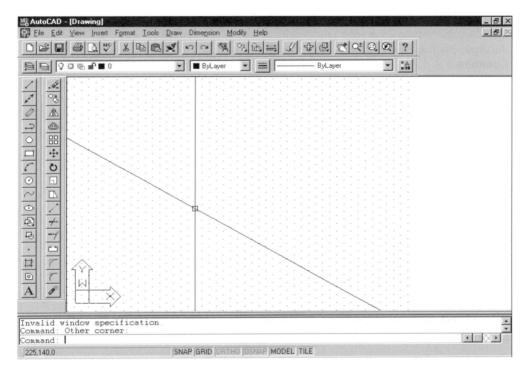

The isoplanes

An isometric circle is drawn as an ellipse (called an **isocircle**). When the **Ellipse** tool is called, with **Snap** set to the **Isometric** style, the Command Line shows:

Command:_ellipse
Arc/Center/Isocircle/<Axis endpoint 1>:

According to which isoplane is active, the ellipse will be drawn at the correct isometric angle. To draw an isocircle call **Ellipse**:

Command: _ellipse
Arc/Center/Isocircle/<Axis endpoint 1>: *enter* i *right-click*
Center of circle: *pick* or *enter* coordinates
<Circle radius>/Diameter: *pick* or *enter* coordinates
Command:

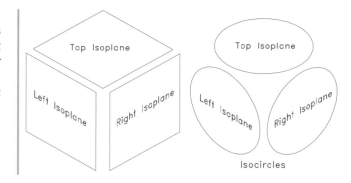

Isocircles

☐ **EXAMPLE 1** ☐

1 Open your drawing template
2 **Command: _snap**
   Snap spacing or ON/OFF/Aspect/Rotate/Style<5>: *enter* s *right-click*
   Standard/Isometric <5>: *enter* i *right-click*
   Vertical spacing <5>: *right-click*
   Command:

3 Press the **F7** key to set **Grid** 'on'.
4 Press **Ctrl+E** until the **Top** isoplane is current.
5 Call **Line**. Start a line at 147,205, and draw an isometric rectangle 170 by 120.
6 Press **Ctrl+E** until the **Left** isoplane is current.
7 Draw an isometric rectangle, to fit against the top line, of height 70.
8 Press **Ctrl+E** until the **Top** isoplane is current.
9 Draw an isometric rectangle of 60 wide to fit against the vertical isometric rectangle.
10 Press **Ctrl+E** until the **Right** isoplane is current.
11 Draw an isometric rectangle of height 40 to fit against the last horizontal rectangle.
12 Press **Ctrl+E** until the **Right** isoplane is current.
13 Complete the outline as shown.
14 Press **Ctrl+E** until the **Top** isoplane is current.
15 Call **Ellipse**:

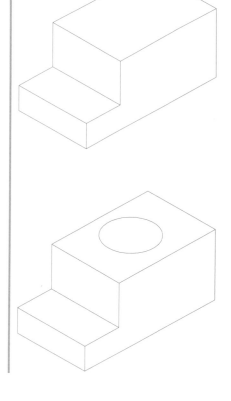

Command: _ellipse
Arc/Center/Isocircle/<Axis endpoint 1>: *enter* i *right-click*
Center of circle: *enter* 268,220 *right-click*
<Circle radius>/Diameter: *enter* 40 *right-click*
Command:

□ **EXAMPLE 2** □

1 Set **Isometric Snap/Grid** 'on'.
2 Press **F7** to set **Grid** 'on'.
3 Isoplane **Top**: with **Line** draw an isometric rectangle 150 by 20, by moving the cursors along the isometric angles and *entering* the figures.
4 Isoplane **Right**: draw rectangle 200 by 150.
5 Isoplane **Left**: draw rectangle 200 by 20.
6 Isoplane **Right**: draw rectangle, inset 30 from the 200 by 150 rectangle.
7 Isoplane **Top** and **Left**: add back lines of rectangular hole.
8 With **Polyline Edit** change the width of all outer lines to 1.

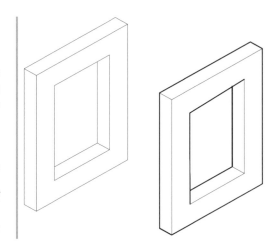

□ **EXAMPLE 3** □

1 Set **Isometric Snap/grid** 'on'.
2 Press **F7** to set **Grid** 'on'.
3 Draw isocircle: centre 242,210; radius 80
4 Call **Copy Object** and copy the isocircle downwards by 40 units.
5 With **Line** add lines as shown.
6 Add a line using the **Qua** osnap points on the two isocircles.
7 Use **Trim** to trim unwanted parts of isocircles.

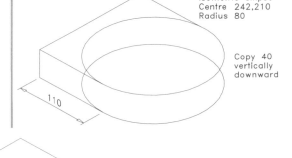

Isometric ellipse
Centre 242,210
Radius 80

Copy 40
vertically
downward

110

8 Draw an isocircle of radius 50 at the centre of the upper isocircle.
9 **Copy** the isocircle by 40 vertically down.

10 Trim unwanted parts of lower isocircle.

11 Copy (with a window) the whole drawing 120 vertically downwards.

12 Trim unwanted parts of the lower copy.

13 With Line add the lines of the back.

14 Use Trim to trim unwanted lines of the back.

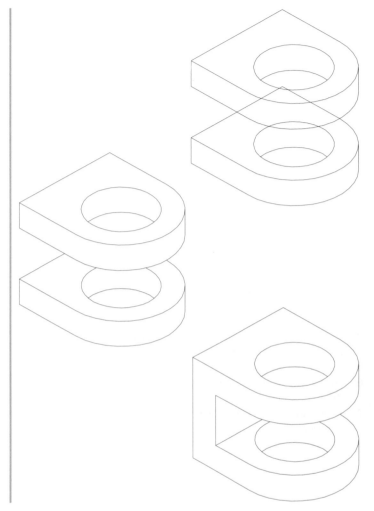

QUESTIONS

1 In **first angle projection**, in which position is the plan of an article placed in relation to the front view of the article?

2 In **third angle projection**, in which position is an end view placed (as seen from the right of the front view of an article) in relation to the front view?

3 Is there a limit to the number of views which can be included in an orthographic projection?

4 How can the cursor in AutoCAD be set for **isometric** drawing?

5 How are **isoplanes** toggled?

6 When drawing an isometric ellipse, what differences are there in the **Ellipse** tool's sequence of prompts?

1 A three-view third angle orthographic projection of an angle bracket is shown (front view, end view and plan).

With **Polyline** (or **Line**), **Circle**, **Trim** and **Fillet**, and working to the given dimensions, construct a first angle three-view orthographic projection of the angle bracket.

Do not include any of the dimensions.

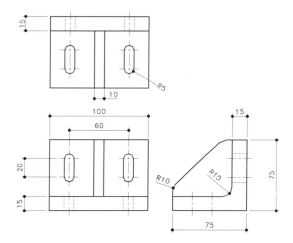

2 A front view and a plan of a fork connector are shown. This drawing could be either in first or third angle projection because the plan would be the same for either form of projection.

Construct a three-view third angle projection of the connector with the aid of **Polyline** (or **Line**), **Circle** and **Fillet**. Do not include any of the dimensions.

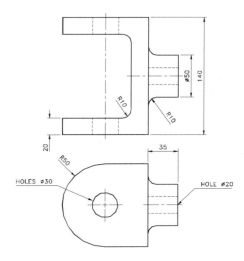

3 A two-view third angle projection of a clip from a machine is shown.

Construct an isometric drawing of the clip.

(This may seem at first glance to be a rather difficult isometric exercise, but if you have worked through the three worked examples given previously the answer should not give too much difficulty.)

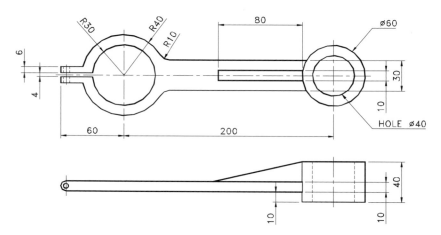

4 A three-view first angle orthographic projection of a slide is given.

Construct an isometric drawing of the slide. Do not include any of the dimensions.

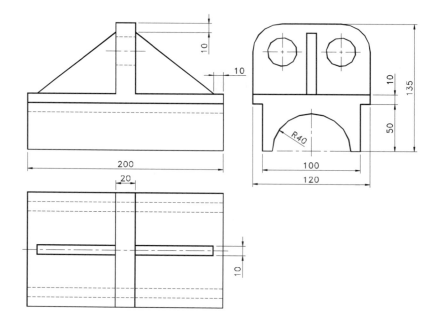

CHAPTER 14

Dimensioning drawings

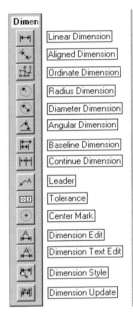

Dimensions are a very important part of a technical drawing. AutoCAD includes a large variety of methods for including dimensions within drawings. The more frequently used methods are shown here. You are advised to experiment with the different types of dimensions available so that, when necessary, a technical drawing can be fully and satisfactorily dimensioned.

In general, there are two ways in which dimensions can be added to drawings:

1 By selection of the appropriate tool from the **Dimensions** toolbar. Each selected tool allows a single dimension to be drawn.
2 By *entering* the command **Dim** at the Command Line. Dimensions can be added one after the other before closing the **Dim** sequences.

☐ **NOTE** ☐

The dimension style for your drawing template has already been set up (Chapter 5).

Adding dimensions using the Command Line

Command: *enter* dim *right-click*
Dim: *enter* hor (horizontal) *right-click*
First extension line origin or press ENTER to select: *pick*
Second extension line origin: *pick*
Dimension text (130): *right-click* (accept) or *enter* new
    dimension
Dim:

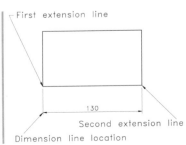

■ Other abbreviations which can be used with Dim

ve vertical
l   leader
ra radius
d   diameter
al aligned
an angular
cen centre mark

Adding dimensions using the toolbar

From the **Toolbars** dialogue box, *left-click* in the check box in front of the name **Dimensions** and the **Dimensions** toolbar appears on screen. Tools for dimensions can then be selected from the toolbar.

When a dimension tool is selected from the toolbar a similar set of prompts appears at the Command Line to when **Dim** is *entered* and followed by a dimension abbreviation.

When adding a horizontal or vertical dimension with the aid of a dimension tool, use **Linear**. The figures for the dimensions automatically line up either horizontally or vertically.

All the dimensions shown in the drawings have been drawn with the dimension styles set in our drawing template (in Chapter 5).

Other set-ups can be used to obtain different styles of dimensioning.

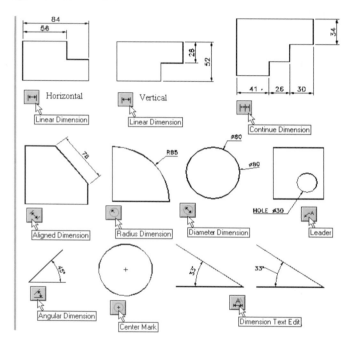

Different dimension styles

Refer to the **Dimension Styles** dialogue boxes. The different methods of dimensioning shown in the next sequence of drawings have been obtained by amending these settings.

The drawings are self-explanatory, but need careful examination. As an exercise, the reader is advised to attempt to create similar forms of dimensions by changing settings in the **Dimension Styles** dialogue boxes.

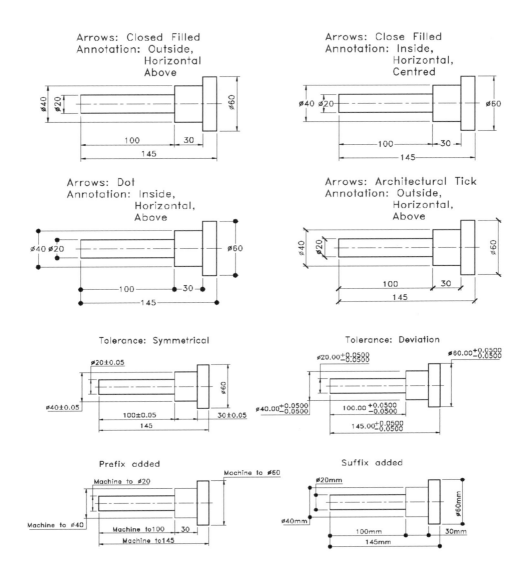

Arrows: Closed Filled
Annotation: Outside,
Horizontal
Above

Arrows: Close Filled
Annotation: Inside,
Horizontal,
Centred

Arrows: Dot
Annotation: Inside,
Horizontal,
Above

Arrows: Architectural Tick
Annotation: Outside,
Horizontal,
Above

Tolerance: Symmetrical

Tolerance: Deviation

Prefix added

Suffix added

□ **EXAMPLE 1** □

1 Open your drawing template.
2 Set both **Grid** (**F7**) and **Snap** (**F9**) 'on'.
3 Working to sizes as shown on the next page, copy both given views, without the dimensions.
4 Select the **Linear Dimension** tool from the **Dimension** toolbar.
5 *Picking* pairs of points in turn (**1** and **2**; **2** and **3**; **4** and **5**; **6** and **7**; **8** and **9**; **9** and **10**; **11** and **12**; **13** and **14**; **15** and **16**) add the linear dimensions to your two views.
6 Select the **Diameter Dimension** tool from the **Dimension** toolbar.
7 *Pick* the left-hand circle to apply the diameter dimension.

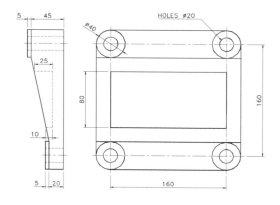

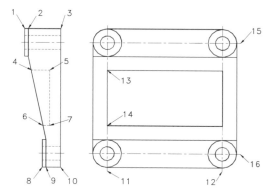

8 Select the **Leader** tool from the **Dimension** toolbar and with the aid of the **Near** osnap *pick* the inner of the two right-hand circles and *enter* **HOLES %%C20** when prompted to do so by **Annotation**.

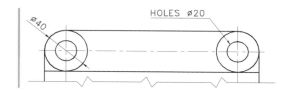

□ **EXAMPLE 2** □

1 Open your drawing template.
2 Set **Grid (F7)** and **Snap (F9)** 'on'.
3 Construct the drawing to the given sizes.
4 Select the **Linear Dimension** tool. *Pick* **A**, then **B**, then the location of the dimension line.
5 Select the **Continue Dimension** tool. *Pick* **C**, then a dimension line location.
6 *Right-click. Pick* **D**, then a dimension line location.
7 *Right-click. Pick* **E**, then a dimension line location.
8 *Right-click. Pick* **F**, then a dimension line location.
9 Select the **Linear Dimension** tool. *Pick* **H**, then **E**, then a dimension line location.
10 *Right-click. Pick* **F**, then **E**, then a dimension line location.
11 Select the **Continue Dimension** tool. *Pick* **G**, then a dimension line location.
12 Select the **Angular Dimension** tool. *Pick* line **HK**, then line **KL**, then a dimension line location.
13 Select the **Diameter Dimension** tool. *Pick* **M**, then a dimension line location.
14 Select the **Radius Dimension** tool. *Pick* **N**, then a dimension line location.

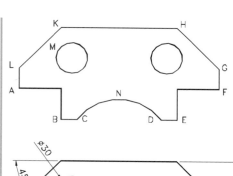

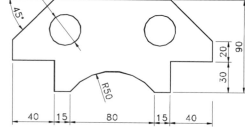

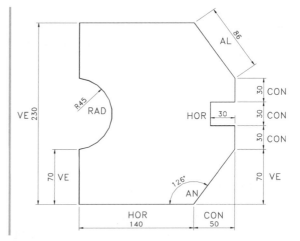

1 Open your drawing template.
2 Construct the drawing to the given sizes.
3 Add dimensions by *entering* **dim** at the Command Line and *entering* the abbreviations as shown next to the given dimensions to draw horizontal (**hor**), vertical (**ve**), aligned (**al**), continue (**con**), radius (**rad**) and angle (**an**) dimensions.

QUESTIONS

1 How are dimension styles set?
2 If you alter the style of text font, does the dimension style also change?
3 What steps are needed before the tolerance ±0.5 can be included with all dimensions added to a drawing?
4 How could the suffix **mm** be included after all dimensions in a drawing?
5 When using the method of dimensioning by *entering* **dim** at the Command Line, to add a horizontal dimension to a drawing the abbreviation **hor** is *entered* at the **Dim:** prompt. How are horizontal dimensions added using a dimension tool from the **Dimensions** toolbar?
6 When using the method of dimensioning by *entering* **dim** at the Command Line, to add a vertical dimension to a drawing the abbreviation **ve** is *entered* at the **Dim:** prompt. How are vertical dimensions added using a dimension tool from the **Dimensions** toolbar?
7 In the first worked example the dimension **HOLES Ø20** was added with the aid of **Leader**. Why not use the **Diameter Dimension** tool for this purpose?
8 When *entering* the dimension **HOLES Ø20**, the diameter symbol was *entered* as **%%C**. How would a degree sign after the figures have been *entered*?
9 In the second worked example the circle is dimensioned with a line and arrows crossing the circle. If you wished to *enter* the dimension **Ø30** without the dimension line crossing the circle, how would you proceed?
10 You have tried two methods of dimensioning – using tools from the **Dimension** toolbar and by *entering* **dim** at the Command Line? There is a third method: *entering* **dim1** at the Command Line; try this out.

EXERCISES

From your floppy disk, open past drawings which have been obtained by answering exercises throughout previous chapters and fully dimension them.

CHAPTER 15

Blocks and Inserts

The Make Block tool

To call the **Make Block** tool, either *left-click* on its icon in the **Draw** toolbar, select **Make...** from the **Block** sub-menu in the **Draw** pull-down menu, or enter **bmake** at the Command Line. No matter which of these alternatives is used, the **Block Definition** dialogue box appears on screen.

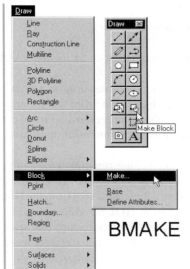

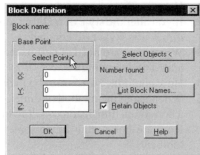

With the aid of the **Make Block** tool any drawing, or part of a drawing, can be inserted into another drawing.

☐ **EXAMPLE** ☐ *making a block*

1 Open your drawing template.
2 Construct a front view of a bolt such as that shown.
3 Call **Make Block**. The **Block Definition** dialogue box appears. In the **Block Name:** box *enter* the name **BOLT**.
4 *Left-click* on the **Select Point** button. The dialogue box disappears.
5 *Left-click* at a selected point (the insertion point) of the bolt drawing. The **Block Definition** dialogue box reappears.

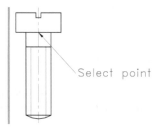

6 *Left-click* on the **Select objects** button:

> **Select objects:** *pick* top left of drawing **Other corner:** *pick* bottom
>   left **7 found**
> **Select objects:** *right-click*
> **Command:**

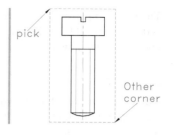

pick

Other corner

7 The **Block Definition** dialogue box reappears. In the **Block Name:** box *enter* the name **BOLT**.

8 *Left-click* on the **OK** button.

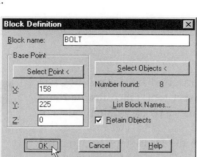

9 If the **Block Definition** dialogue box is brought to screen again (call the tool), a *left-click* on the **List Block Names** button brings up the **Block Names In This Drawing** box. The name **BOLT** should appear in the list.

□ **N O T E** □

Many blocks can be drawn, saved and named in a drawing. When a number have been constructed, all their names will appear in the **Block Names In This Drawing** box. Such blocks can only be inserted into the drawing in which they have been made with **bmake**.

▨ Written blocks (wblocks)

Any part of a drawing may be saved as a separate drawing with the aid of the **wblock** command.

> **Command:** *enter* w (wblock) *right-click*

The **Create Drawing File** dialogue box appears. In the **File Name** box *enter* the required file name, followed by a *left-click* on the **Save** button.

> **Block name:** *right-click* (it has been *entered* in the dialogue box)
> **Insertion base point:** *pick* a suitable point
> **Select objects:** window that part of the drawing to be saved
> **Select objects:** *right-click*
> **Command:**

The selected part of the drawing disappears, but can be made to reappear by *entering* **oops** at the Command Line. The part of the drawing selected has been saved as a separate drawing, under the file name *entered* in the **Create Drawing File** dialogue box.

□ **NOTE** □

Do not confuse **blocks** with **written blocks** (**wblocks**). A block can only exist in the data of the drawing in which it was made. A written block is a new drawing in its own right and is not part of the data of another drawing.

The Insert tool

Any AutoCAD block can be inserted into any AutoCAD drawing with the aid of the **Insert** tool. Once inserted into another drawing the insert becomes a block within the data of the new drawing.

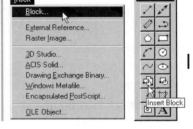

The tool can be called from the **Draw** toolbar, from the **Insert** pull-down menu, or by *entering* **i** at the Command Line.

In the **Insert** dialogue box *left-click* on **File...** and the **Select Drawing File** dialogue box appears, from which a file can be selected.

Select the required file, followed by a *left-click* on the **Open** button of the dialogue box; the full file name appears in the **File...** box of the **Insert** dialogue box.

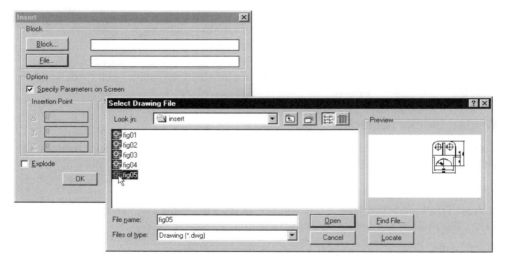

Left-click on the **OK** button of the dialogue box and the selected file appears in 'ghost' form in the AutoCAD window. It can now be *dragged* by its insertion point anywhere on screen.

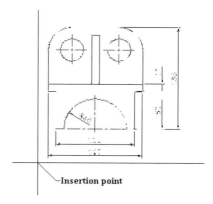

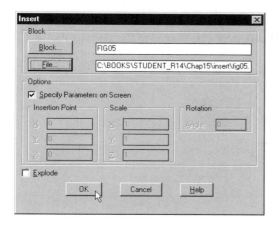

—Insertion point

The Command Line then shows:

Insertion point: *pick* a suitable point
X scale factor <1>/Corner/XYZ: *right-click* or *enter* a scale number
Y scale factor <default = X>: *right-click*
Rotation angle: *right-click* or *enter* a rotation angle
Command:

☐ EXAMPLE 1 ☐

Use the block already constructed (on page 104); either **Insert** it as a block or, having previously saved it as a wblock, **Insert** it as a drawing from a file. The results of different **X** and **Y** factors and **Rotation** angles are shown below.

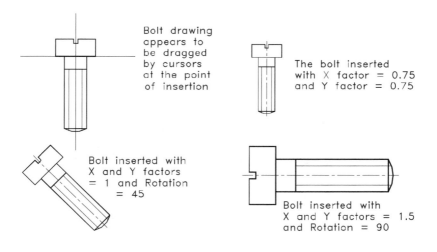

Bolt drawing appears to be dragged by cursors at the point of insertion

The bolt inserted with X factor = 0.75 and Y factor = 0.75

Bolt inserted with X and Y factors = 1 and Rotation = 45

Bolt inserted with X and Y factors = 1.5 and Rotation = 90

1 The given drawings of a **BOLT01** and **HEAD** were constructed to the sizes as shown and then saved as blocks.

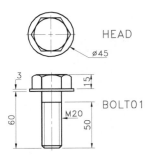

2 A two-view orthographic projection of a clutch was drawn.

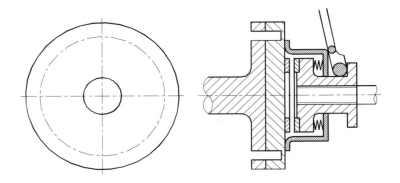

3 The two blocks were then inserted as shown in the drawing below.

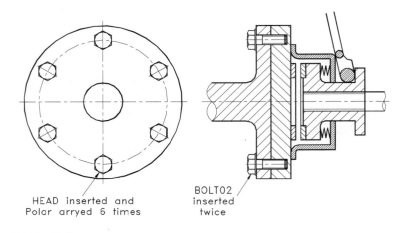

HEAD inserted and
Polar arryed 6 times

BOLT02
inserted
twice

□ **EXAMPLE 3** □ *an electric circuit*

The making and insertion of blocks is of particular value when constructing any form of circuit diagram (electrical, electronic, pneumatic, hydraulic, etc.) since any form of circuit diagram requires the use of repeating symbols. This example is of a simple electronics diagram.

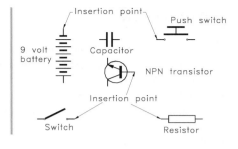

1 Construct the six electronic/electrical symbols as shown and save each symbol as a wblock.
2 **Insert** the symbols in their approximate positions relative to each other, as shown.
3 **Rotate** and/or **Move** those symbols required to be placed more precisely or in a different orientation.

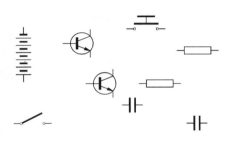
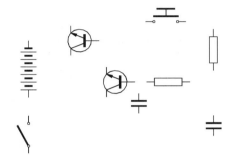

4 Add conductor lines between the symbols to complete the circuit diagram.
5 Add descriptive labels to the symbols. Call the **Donut** tool and add donuts of **Inside diameter** 0 and **Outside diameter** 3 at the intersecting points of the conductor lines.

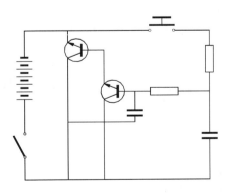
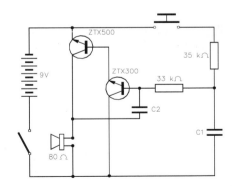

1 There are two basic types of blocks. Can you describe them?
2 What do you think is meant by a **library of symbols** when using CAD software such as AutoCAD?
3 Blocks are usually inserted as single objects, no matter how many objects they actually contain. A single object block can be exploded into its various separate objects. Can you explain how this is carried out?
4 What is the purpose of the **Insertion point** of a block?
5 Why is it important to make sure the **Insertion point** is chosen carefully?

EXERCISES

1 Working to any convenient sizes, construct blocks for a resistor, an NPN transistor and a diode. Insert the blocks you have drawn into the circuit as shown.

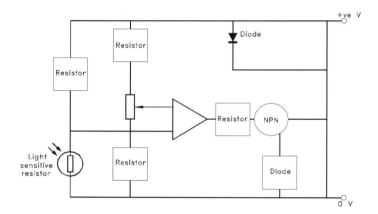

2 Construct further blocks for a capacitor and a 9-volt battery. Then insert these blocks and those from Exercise 1 to construct the circuit as shown.

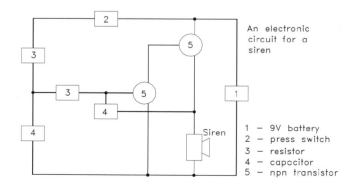

CHAPTER 16

3D drawing with Solids tools

The Solids toolbar

Right-click anywhere in any toolbar on screen (except in a tool icon) to bring up the **Toolbars** dialogue box. *Left-click* in the check box against the name **Solids** to bring the **Solids** toolbar on screen. Close the **Toolbars** dialogue box.

While working on the examples and exercises in this chapter *drag* the toolbar to the right-hand side of the AutoCAD window to *dock* it against that side.

The UCS

The **User Coordinate System** (UCS) is essential to the construction of 3D solid models in AutoCAD. We have so far been working in the default **World Coordinate System** (WCS). The UCS allows the operator to work with the coordinate system laid out in any position relative to the views drawn in the WCS – from the sides, from the front, from the top, from the bottom or, in fact, from any other angle.

■ The UCSfollow set variable

AutoCAD is controlled by a series of **set variables**. We have not referred to these yet because we have accepted AutoCAD's default set variables. The UCS cannot be changed unless the set variable **UCSfollow** is set 'on' (that is to 1):

> **Command:** *enter* ucsfollow *right-click*
> **New value for UCSFOLLOW <0>:** *enter* 1 *right-click*
> **Command:**

It is advisable at this stage to resave your drawing template in order to include this setting within the template.

■ UCS Orientation dialogue box

The easiest method of obtaining a new UCS is to call the **UCS Orientation** dialogue box with a *left-click* on **Preset UCS...** from the **UCS** sub-menu in the **Tools** pull-down menu.

As can be seen in the dialogue box, the **User Coordinate System** can be set to allow a 3D model to be viewed from **Top**, **Back**, **Left**, **Front**, **Right** or **Bottom**.

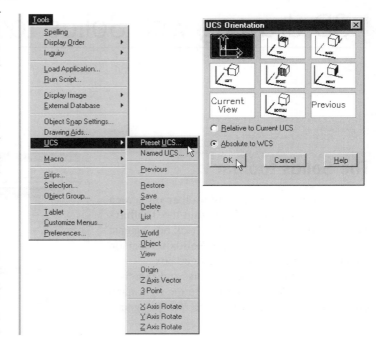

□ **NOTE** □

There are two radio buttons above the **OK** button. It is usually best to make sure that **Absolute to WCS** is set 'on' (dot within circle) when working through the examples and exercises in this book.

□ **EXAMPLE 1** □

1 Open your drawing template.
2 Set **UCSfollow** to **1**.
3 Save your drawing template to the same file name used originally.
4 Press **F7** to set **Grid** 'on'. Make sure **Snap** is also set 'on'.
5 From the **UCS Orientation** dialogue box, set the UCS to **RIGHT** – *double-click* on the **RIGHT** icon in the dialogue box.
6 **Command:** *enter* z (zoom) *right-click*
   All/Center/Dynamic/Extents/Previous/Scale(X/XP)/
      Window/<Realtime>: *enter* 1 *right-click*
   Command:

   Note the grid system changes to the scale at which **Limits** were set in your drawing template.
7 Construct the outline as shown, with the aid of the **Polyline** tool without the dimensions. Make sure your pline is a closed pline by using **C** to close the last line of the outline.
8 Call the **Extrude** tool from the **Solids** toolbar, or *enter* **ext** at the Command Line:

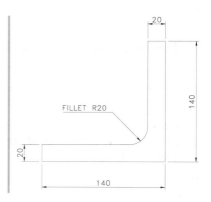

Command: _extrude
Select objects: *pick* the outline **1 found**
Select objects: *right-click*
Path <Height of Extrusion>: *enter* 100 *right-click*
Extrusion taper angle<0>: *right-click*
Command:

9   In the **View** pull-down menu *left-click* on **SE Isometric** in the **3D Viewpoint** sub-menu. The 3D solid model just extruded appears in an isometric view (as seen from the South East relative to the WCS).

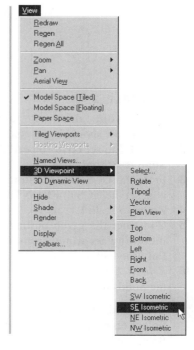

10 **Command:** *enter* hi (hide) *right-click*
   HIDE Regenerating drawing.
   Command:

Lines behind the front edges of the model are hidden.

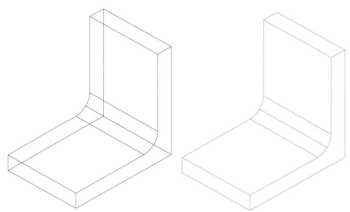

11 Select the **Chamfer** tool from the **Modify** toolbar.

Command: _chamfer
(TRIM mode) Current chamfer Dist1 = 10, Dist2 = 10
Polyline/Distance/Angle/Trim/Method/<Select first line>: *enter* d *right-click*
Enter first chamfer distance <10>: *enter* 20 *right-click*
Enter second chamfer distance <20>: *right-click*
Command: *right-click*
(TRIM mode) Current chamfer Dist1 = 20, Dist2 = 20
Polyline/Distance/Angle/Trim/Method/<Select first line>: *pick* a corner line
Select base surface:

3D drawing with Solids tools ■ **113**

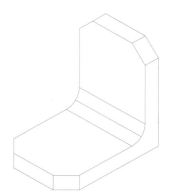

Next/<OK>: *right-click*
Enter base surface distance <20>: *right-click*
Enter other surface distance <20>: *right-click*
Loop/<Select edge>: *pick* the edge again
Loop/<Select edge>: *right-click*
Command:

Chamfer each edge in turn.

□ **EXAMPLE 2** □

1 Open your drawing template.
   UCSfollow should be set 'on'.
2 Press **F7** to set **Grid** 'on'. Make sure
   Snap is set 'on'.
3 From the **UCS Orientation** dialogue
   box, set the UCS to **FRONT**.
4 **Zoom** to scale **1**.
5 Construct the given outline without
   including its dimensions. Use the
   Polyline tool and close the outline.
6 *Left-click* on the **Revolve** tool icon in
   the **Solids** toolbar:

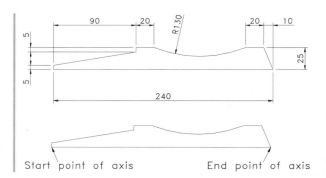

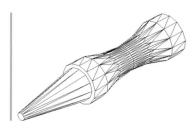

   Command: _revolve
   Select objects: *pick* the polyline **1 found**
   Select objects: *right-click*
   Axis of revolution – Object/X/Y/<Start point of axis>: *pick*
   <End point of axis>: *pick*
   Angle of revolution <full circle>: *right-click*
   Command:

7 Place in the **SW Isometric** view.
8 Call **Hide** to regenerate the drawing.

□ **EXAMPLE 3** □

1 **Open** your drawing template.
2 Press **F7** to set **Grid** 'on'. Make sure **Snap** is set 'on'.
3 *Left-click* on **Box** in the **Solids** toolbar:

   Command: _box
   Center/<Corner of box>: *enter* 150,130
   Cube/Length/<Other corner>: *enter* 370,90
   Height: *enter* 100
   Command:

4 *Left-click* on **Cylinder** in the **Solids** toolbar:

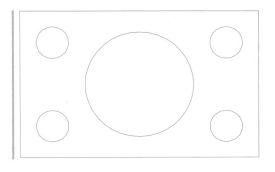

Command: _cylinder
Elliptical/<Center point><0,0,0>: *enter*
   260,160,100 *right-click*
Diameter/<Radius>: *enter* 50 *right-click*
Center of other end/<Height>: *enter* 100
Command: *right-click*
Command: _cylinder
Elliptical/<Center point><0,0,0>: *enter*
   340,200 *right-click*
Diameter/<Radius>: *enter* 15 *right-click*
Center of other end/<Height>: *enter* 100
Command: *enter* cp *right-click*
Select objects: *pick* the small cylinder **1 found**
Select objects: *right-click*
<Base point or displacement>/Multiple: *enter* m *right-click*
Base point: *pick* centre of small cylinder
Second point of displacement: *pick* 180,200 **Second point of displacement:** *pick*
   180,120 **Second point of displacement:** *pick* 340,120 **Second point of**
   displacement: *right-click*
Command:

5 Place in the **SW Isometric** view.
6 *Left-click* on **Union** in the **Boolean** sub-menu of the **Modify** pull-
down menu, or *enter* **uni** at the Command Line:

Command: _union
Select objects: *pick* the box **1 found**
Select objects: *pick* the large cylinder **1 found**
Select objects: *right-click*
Command:

The box and large cylinder are joined together as one unit.
7 *Left-click* on **Subtract** in the **Boolean** sub-menu:

Command: _subtract Select solids and regions to subtract from...
Select objects: *pick* the box and cylinder union **1 found**
Select objects: *right-click*
Select solids and regions to subtract: *pick* one of the small cylinders
   1 found
Select solids and regions to subtract: *pick* another of the small
   cylinders **1 found**
Select solids and regions to subtract: *pick* another of the small
   cylinders **1 found**
Select solids and regions to subtract: *pick* the last of the small cylinders **1 found**
Select solids and regions to subtract: *right-click*
Command:

The smaller cylinders have been subtracted from the box and cylinder union

8   Call **Hide**.
9   Call **Chamfer**. Set **Dist1** and **Dist2** to 10. At the line:

Select base surface:
Next/<OK>: *enter* n *right-click*
Next/<OK>: *right-click* when top surface of box is highlighted.

Then, at the line:

Loop/<Select edge>: *enter* I *right-click* and *pick* the highlighted edge.

10 **Chamfer** the top edge of the cylinder.
11 Call **Hide** again.

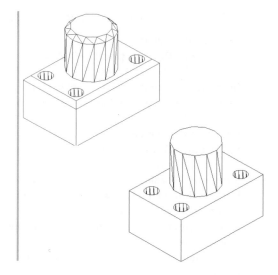

☐   **EXAMPLE 4** ☐

1   Open your drawing template.
2   Press **F7** to set **Grid** 'on'. Make sure **Snap** is set 'on'.
3   **Cone** from **Solids**: centre 260,160; radius 80; height 120.
4   **Sphere** from **Solids**: centre 260,160,80; radius 60.
5   **Union** the two solids.
6   Place in **SW Isometric**.
7   **Hide**.

☐   **EXAMPLE 5** ☐

1   Open your drawing template.
2   Press **F7** to set **Grid** 'on'. Make sure **Snap** is set 'on'.
3   In the **WCS** construct a cylinder: radius 70; height 150.
4   *Left-click* on **Torus** in the **Solids** toolbar:

Command: _torus
Center of torus: *enter* .xy **xy of:** *pick* torus centre
(need Z): *enter* 50 *right-click*
Diameter/<Radius of torus>: *enter* 70 *right-click*
Diameter/<Radius of tube>: *enter* 10 *right-click*
Command:

5   Create a second torus of the same radii at a height of 100, centred on the cylinder.
6   Place in **NW Isometric** view.
7   **Union** cylinder and lower torus.
8   **Subtract** top torus from cylinder.
9   **Fillet** top edge of cylinder to radius 20.
10 **Hide**.

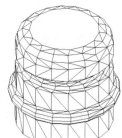

1   How would you call the **Solids** toolbar to screen?
2   What does the abbreviation **UCS** stand for?
3   What is the purpose of the **UCS**?
4   Why is it necessary to set the variable **UCSfollow** 'on' (to 1) when constructing 3D solid models?
5   Have you tried constructing an elliptical cylinder?

EXERCISES

1   The upper drawing is a two-view third angle orthographic drawing of a clip plate from a machine. The lower is a 3D solid model drawing of the plate. Construct the 3D solid model.

   Start with the top of the plate, making sure its outline is a closed pline; **Extrude** this by 10. Place cylinders at the hole positions and **Subtract** them from the plate.

   Place in **Front UCS** and **Zoom** to **1**.

   Construct one of the flanges (**Extrude** outline and **Subtract** hole). In the **WCS**, move flange to correct position in relation to top plate and **Copy** to other side. Finally place in **SW Isometric** and use **Hide**.

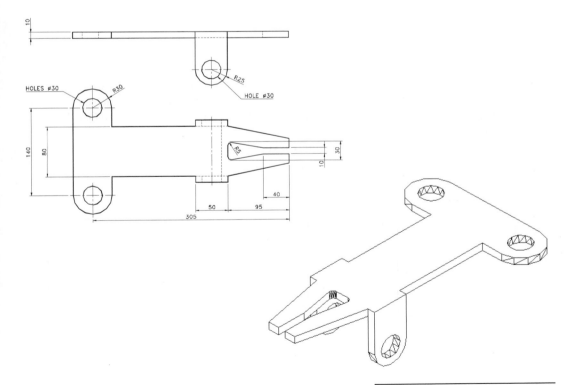

2 The upper drawing shows a part from a machine in a two-view first angle orthographic projection. Construct the 3D solid model drawing of the part as shown in the lower drawing. In the **FRONT** UCS construct two cylinders and **Subtract** the inner from the outer. Then construct the top most vertical fin with the aid of the **Polyline** tool (the outline must be closed). **Extrude** the fin outline to 50.

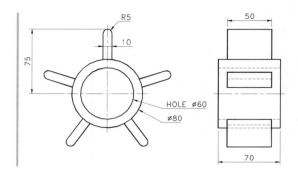

Change to the **RIGHT** UCS and move the fin to its correct position; change back to the **FRONT** UCS. Polar **Array** the fin around the centre of the tube five times and then **Union** the six parts together. Finally place in **SW Isometric** view and call **Hide**.

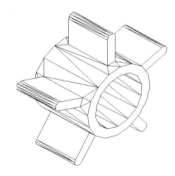

3 Construct a 3D solid model of the part shown in the two-view first angle projection.

Start in the **FRONT** UCS with the end view, followed by **Extrude**; **Subtract** the Ø20 hole from the extrusion. Then use **Chamfer**. In the **RIGHT** UCS subtract the Ø10 holes from the extrusion.

The given 3D model is on the **SW Isometric** view.

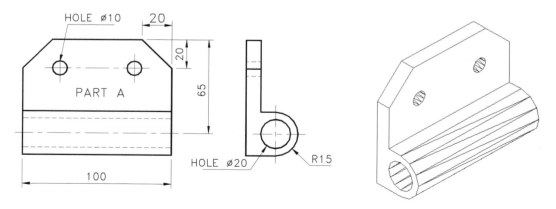

CHAPTER 17

More Solids tools

□ **EXAMPLE 1** □

1 Open your drawing template.
2 Work to the sizes given in the drawing.
3 **Extrude** a base from a closed polyline and **Subtract** from the base four cylinders for the holes in the base.

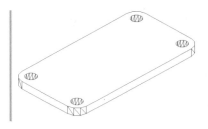

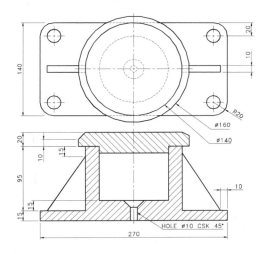

4 Construct a cylinder of Ø100 and height 80 and one of Ø140 and height 95.
5 With **Union** join the cylinders to the base.

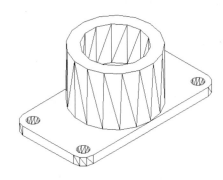

6 In the centre of the base **Subtract** a cylinder unioned with a cone to form the countersunk hole in the base. This is not shown here.

7 In the **FRONT** UCS construct pline outlines for the webs and **Extrude** to 10 high.

8 In the **WCS**, with the aid of **Move**, move the two webs into their correct position.

9 In the **FRONT** UCS construct a polyline outline around which the cap can be revolved.

10 With **Revolve** form a solid of revolution from the polyline.

11 In the **WCS** move the cap into its correct position.

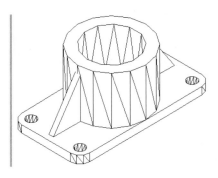

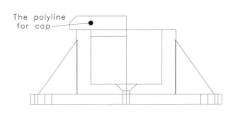

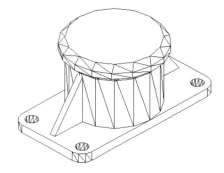

□ **EXAMPLE 2** □

1 Place the 3D solid model from the first worked example in the **WCS**.

2 *Left-click* on **Slice** in the **Solids** toolbar:

Command: _slice
Select objects: *pick* both parts of the 3D solid model
Select objects: *right-click*
Slicing plane by Object/ZAxis/View/XY/YZ/ZX/<3points>: *right-click*
1st point on plane: *pick*
2nd point on plane: *pick*
3rd point on plane: *enter* .xy **xy of:** *pick* 1st point again
(need Z): *enter* 1 *right-click*
Both sides/<Point on desired side of plane>: point by *picking*
Command:

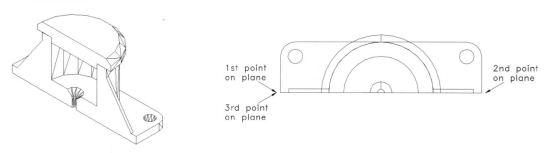

□ EXAMPLE 3 □

1 Place the 3D model drawing from the second worked example in the **WCS**.
2 **Erase** the cap.
3 *Left-click* on **Section** in the **Solids** toolbar:

Command: _section
Select objects: *pick* the 3D solid model

The same prompts appear as when using the **Slice** tool for three points on the section plane.
4 In the **FRONT** UCS hatch the surface formed by the **Surface** tool – use **ANSI31** at **Scale** 2 and **Angle** 0.
5 Place in **SE Isometric** view to see the section.

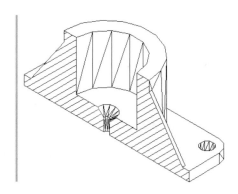

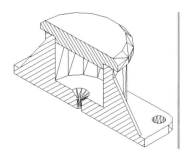

□ NOTES □

1 When using the filter **.xy** and **(need Z)** is prompted, it is only the direction of the **Z** axis which is required, therefore the figure **1** is quite sufficient to set the plane in its required position.
2 Try sectioning the cap of the solid; it must be treated as a separate object and the hatching should be at 90° to allow the hatching to be at the opposite angle to that of the other part of the model.

□ EXAMPLE 4 □

The drawing to the right is a four-view third angle orthographic projection of an electric probe.

This example is based upon the details given in this drawing.

1 Open your drawing template.
2 Check that **Grid** and **Snap** are 'on'.
3 Construct a closed polyline as shown (left).
4 Call the **Revolve** tool from **Solids** and form the solid of revolution of the polyline.
5 Construct a closed polyline for the probe part of the article (right).

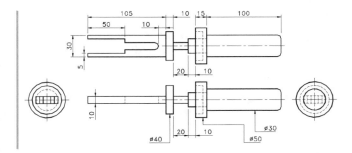

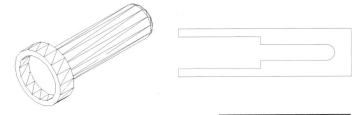

6 **Extrude** the polyline to a height of 10.

7 In the **RIGHT** UCS construct three cylinders to form the part joining the handle to the probe. Use the **Union** tool to join the three together. It may be necessary to place the three cylinders in the **WCS** to move the parts to their required positions relative to each other.

8 In the **WCS**, with the aid of the **Move** tool, move the three parts together into their correct positions and join them using the **Union** tool.

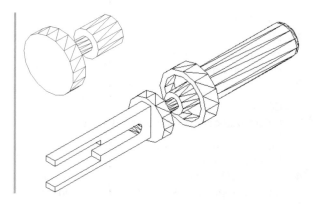

☐ **EXAMPLE 5** ☐

1 With the fourth worked example on screen, call **Regen**:

Command: *enter* re *right-click*
Regenerating drawing:
Command:

2 *Left-click* on **Paper Space** in the **View** pull-down menu. The screen changes. The UCS icon is replaced by the Paper Space icon and the drawing no longer appears on screen.

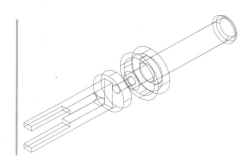

3 **Command:** *enter* mview *right-click*
ON/OFF/Hideplot/Fit/2/3/4/Restore/<First point>: *enter* f
      right-click
Regenerating drawing:
Command:

The drawing reappears.

4 **Command:** *enter* ms (Model Space) *right-click*
MSPACE
Command:

5 *Left-click* on the **Setup Profile** tool icon in the **Solids** toolbar:

Command: _solprof
Select objects: *pick* the model
Select objects: *right-click*
Display hidden profile lines on separate layer? <Y>: *right-click*
Project profile lines onto a plane <Y>: *right-click*
Delete tangential edges <Y>: *right-click*
One solid selected:
Command:

6 *Left-click* on the **Layers** icon in the **Object Properties** toolbar at top of the screen. The **Layer & Linetype** dialogue box appears. New layers with names commencing with **Ph** and **Pv**, each followed by a number, will be seen in the dialogue box. Turn off layer **0** and the layer commencing with **Ph**. Make layer **Pv** current. *Left-click* on the **OK** button of the dialogue box.

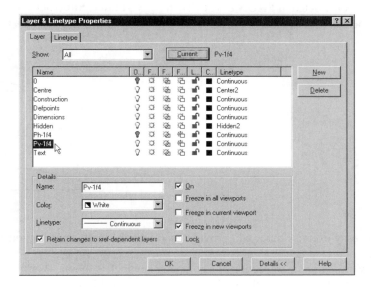

The 3D solid model drawing appears in the AutoCAD window in profile only. The resulting profiled 3D solid model is shown on the right.

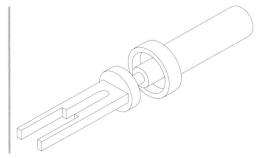

QUESTIONS

1 What is the purpose of the **Boolean** operator known as the **Union** tool?

2 Which side of a view should the operator select when using the **Slice** tool to remove part of a 3D solid model?

3 Can a sectional view obtained from a 3D solid model be moved away from the solid model? Have you tried to do so?

4 What is the purpose of the filter **.xy**?

5 Why is it only necessary to *enter* **1** when setting the **Z** axis position in answer to the **3points** prompt of the **Section** and **Slice** tools?

6 What is the purpose of the **Setup Profile** tool?

1   A two-view projection of a rotating link from a machine is given.
    Construct the 3D solid model profile for the link as shown. Use the tools **Polyline,
Circle** and **Trim** to construct the outline for the extrusions of base and web. The web
will need to be constructed in **FRONT** UCS. Then use **Cylinder**, **Subtract** and **Union**
to complete the solid model. Place the model in a good viewing position, such as **SW
Isometric**.

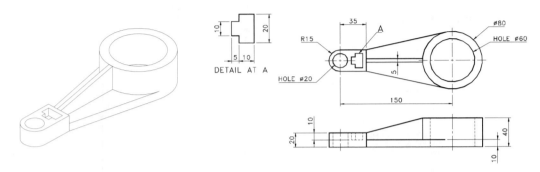

2   This is not an easy exercise but it will provide good practice in the construction of 3D
    solid models.
    A two-view orthographic projection of a computer key lock is shown. Working to the
sizes shown, construct a profile 3D solid model drawing of the key.

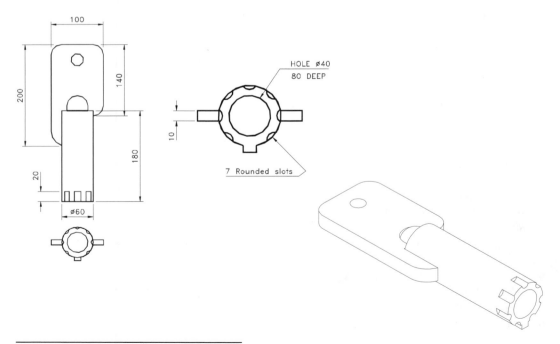

CHAPTER 18

Surfaces tools

To bring the **Surfaces** toolbar on screen, *right-click* in an area of any toolbar already on screen (except on an icon). In the **Toolbars** dialogue box *left-click* in the **Surfaces** check box to bring the toolbar on screen. Only a selection of the **Surfaces** tools will be described in this chapter.

☐ **EXAMPLE 1** ☐ *dome*

1 Open your drawing template.
2 *Left-click* on the **Dome** tool icon in the **Surfaces** toolbar:

> **Command:** _ai_dome
> **Center of dome:** *enter* 260,160
> *right-click*
> **Diameter/<Radius>:** *enter* 100
> *right-click*
> **Number of longitudinal segments**
> **<16>:** *enter* 32 *right-click*
> **Number of latitudinal segments**
> **<8>:** *enter* 16 *right-click*
> **Command:**

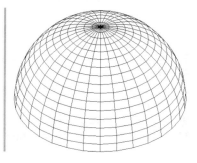

3 Place in the **SW Isometric** view.
4 Call **Hide**.

☐ **EXAMPLE 2** ☐ *dish*

1 Open your drawing template.
2 *Left-click* on the **Dish** tool icon in the **Surfaces** toolbar:

Command: _ai_dome
Center of dome: *enter* 260,160 *right-click*
Diameter/<Radius>: *enter* 100 *right-click*
Number of longitudinal segments <16>: *enter* 32 *right-click*
Number of latitudinal segments <8>: *enter* 16 *right-click*
Command:

3 Place in the **SW Isometric** view.
4 Call **Hide**.

☐ **EXAMPLE 3** ☐ *tabulated surface*

1 Open your drawing template.

2 Construct the polyline as shown.

3 Draw a **Line** from 170,40 to 170,40,150 (note you will not see this line yet).

4 Place in **SW Isometric** view.

5 *Left-click* on the **Tabulated Surface** tool icon in the **Surfaces** toolbar:

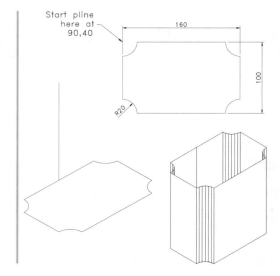

Command: _tabsurf
Select path curve: *pick* the pline outline
Select direction vector: *pick* the vertical line.
Command:

6 Call **Hide**.

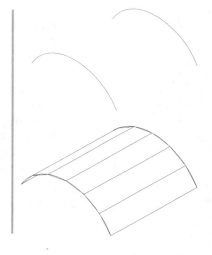

☐ **EXAMPLE 4** ☐ *ruled surface*

1 Open your drawing template.

2 Set **Grid** 'on'.

3 Place in **RIGHT** UCS and **Zoom** to **1**.

4 Construct an arc from 10,10 to 110,70 to 220,10.

5 Place in the **WCS**. The arc will now appear as a line.

6 **Zoom** to **All**.

7 **Move** the arc so that its upper end is at 120,240.

8 **Copy** the arc to 200 to the right.

9 Place in **SW Isometric** view.

10 *Left-click* on the **Ruled Surface** tool icon in the **Surfaces** toolbar.

Command: _rulesurf
Select first defining curve: *pick* one of the arcs
Select second defining curve: *pick* the other arc
Command:

☐ **EXAMPLE 5** ☐ *surftab1*

1 Set the set variable **surftab1** to 32:

Command: *enter* surftab1 *right-click*
New value for SURFTAB1 <6>: *enter* 32 *right-click*
Command:

2 Now **Erase** the ruled surface between the two arcs and call **Ruled Surface** again, followed by *picking* the two arcs.

□ **EXAMPLE 6** □ *edge surface*

1 Open your drawing template.
2 Place plane in the **RIGHT** UCS and **Zoom** to **1**.
3 Construct an arc from 50,100 to 10,10 to 50,-90.
4 Place plane in the **WCS** and **Move** the arc to a more convenient position.
5 **Copy** the arc such that the two arcs are 250 apart.
6 Construct an arc using the End osnap between the two arcs already drawn.
7 Change to the **FRONT** UCS and using the End osnap, **Copy** the arc just drawn to the other ends of the first pair of arcs.
8 Place in **NW Isometric** view.
9 *Left-click* on the **Edge Surface** tool icon in the **Surfaces** toolbar:

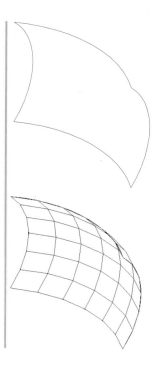

Command: _edgesurf
Select edge 1: *pick* one of the edges
Select edge 2: *pick* a second edge
Select edge 3: *pick* a third edge
Select edge 4: *pick* the last edge
Command:

10 Now set **surftab1** to 16 and **surftab2** to 16 and call **Edge Surface** again.

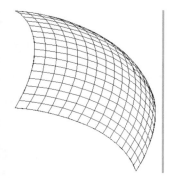

□ **NOTES** □

1 It has already been seen that the density of the mesh drawn using **Surfaces** tools is determined by the setting of the variables **surftab1** and **surftab2**. It is advisable to practise using the **Surfaces** tools with varying **surftab** settings.
2 When using the **Surfaces** tools, it must be remembered that surfaces are produced. This is the major difference between using the **Surfaces** tools as distinct from constructing with the **Solids** tools.

QUESTIONS

1 What is the purpose of the set variable **surftab1**?
2 Have you tried using the **Box**, **Wedge**, **Pyramid**, **Cone** and **Sphere** tools?
3 What is the result if, when using the **Edgesurf** tool, the ends of the four edges do not meet accurately?
4 Can a **Tabulated Surface** be constructed if the direction vector is an arc?
5 Can a **Tabulated Surface** be constructed if the direction vector is a sloping line?

6 When constructing an **Edge Surface** does the setting of **surftab2** affect the mesh of the surface?

1 Construct a **Tabulated Surface** to the shape and sizes as shown.

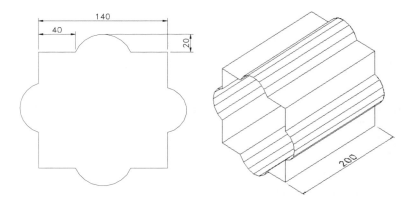

2 The drawing (right) shows a **Dome** resting on an **Edge Surface** constructed on four equal arcs. Working to sizes of your own choice, construct a similar pair of surfaces.

3 The dimensions view (below) shows the basic sizes and shapes on which the 3D surface model shown below has been based. All the surfaces of the model are **Edge Surfaces**.

Construct a similar set of surfaces to form the model as shown.

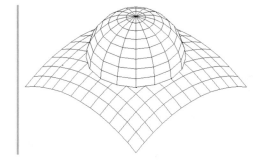

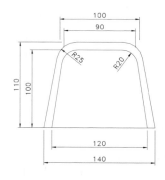

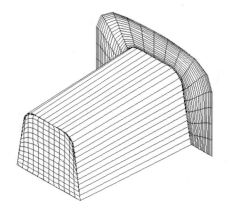

CHAPTER 19

Printing and plotting

It is assumed that readers will be using a computer already set up to print or plot to a default printer or plotter. In many cases this will be the default Windows 95 printer used for the printing from applications other than AutoCAD.

No matter whether the drawing is to be printed or plotted, the same tool and methods are used.

The Print tool

The drawing used to illustrate the method of printing or plotting a drawing is shown below. This is the same 3D solid model profile that was shown on page 124.

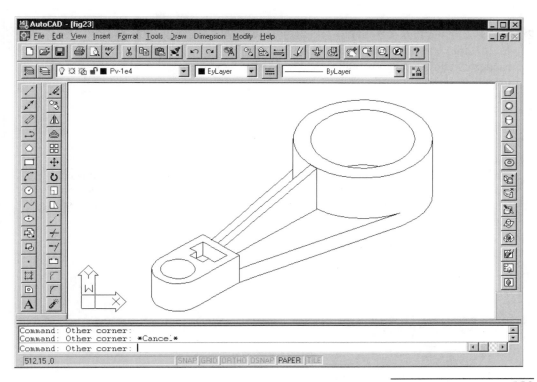

The tool can be called either from the **File** pull-down menu, from the **Print** tool in the **Standard** toolbar, or by *entering* **plot** at the Command Line.

When the tool is called the **Print / Plot Configuration** dialogue box appears on screen.

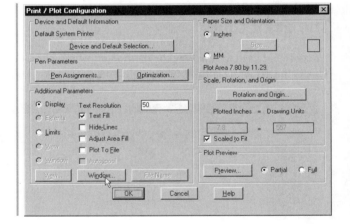

□ **NOTE** □

If the dialogue box does not appear it is because the set variable **CMDDIA** has not been set 'on' (to 1). To set this variable:

Command: *enter* cmddia *right-click*
New value for CMMDIA <0>: *enter* 1 *right-click*
Command:

■ Print configuration

As can be seen in the dialogue box, a variety of settings can be made:

1 *Left-click* on the **Window...** button. The **Window Selection** box appears.
2 *Left-click* on the **Pick <** button in the dialogue box. The box disappears allowing the operator to window the area of the drawing to be printed.
3 The **Window Selection** box reappears displaying the coordinates of the corners of the windowed area.
4 *Left-click* on the **OK** button and the **Print / Plot Configuration** dialogue box reappears. *Left-click* the **Full** radio button in the **Preview** area of the dialogue box followed by another on the **Preview** button. A preview of the drawing as it will appear when printed or plotted appears on screen.

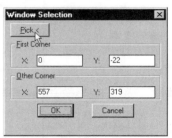

---

130 ■ AutoCAD Release 14: A Concise Guide

5 *Right-click* near the icon in the **Preview** window and again on **Exit** in the pull-down menu. The **Print / Plot Configuration** box reappears. *Left-click* on the **OK** button of the dialogue box – the drawing prints (or plots).

6 If there is any printing problem a warning box comes on screen.

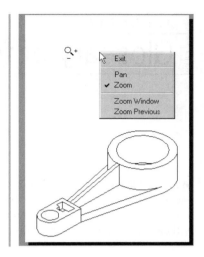

□ **NOTE** □

It will be seen from the **Preview** of this drawing that the drawing could have been better orientated to fill the sheet.

Left-click on the **Rotation and Origin** button in the **Print / Plot Configuration** dialogue box and, in the dialogue which appears, *left-click* in the **90** radio button.

Now when the **Preview** is brought on screen you will see that a better position for the drawing has been achieved.

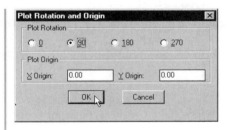

EXERCISES

Load any of the drawings you have created doing the exercises and obtain printouts of them. Such printouts are often referred to as **hardcopy**.

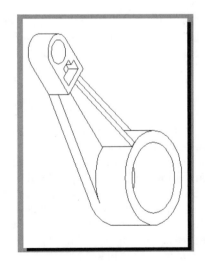

Glossary of tools

Many of the tools (or commands) shown in this glossary have not been described in the pages of this book. This book is intended for those new to AutoCAD Release 14 and only those tools considered essential for the beginner have been included. It is hoped this glossary will encourage readers to experiment with those tools (commands) not described.

☐ NOTES ☐

1 The letters in brackets after the tool name show the abbreviation or key board short-cuts for the tool.

2 The tools printed in bold (e.g. **Array**) are those which have been covered within this book.

3Darray   Creates an array of 3D models in 3D space.

3Dface (3f)   Creates a three- or four-sided 3D mesh behind which other features can be hidden.

3Dmesh   Creates a 3D mesh in 3D space.

3DSin   Brings the **3D Studio File Import** dialogue box on screen.

3DSout   Brings the **3D Studio Output File** dialogue box on screen.

About   Brings the **About AutoCAD** bitmap on screen.

ACSin   Imports an ACIS file into AutoCAD.

ACSout   Exports 3D solid models to ACIS file format.

Align   Allows selected entities to be aligned to selected points in 3D space.

AMEconvert   Converts AME solid models (from Release 12) into Release 14 solid models.

Appload   Brings the **Load AutoLISP, ADS and ARX files** dialogue box on screen.

Arc (a)   Creates an arc.

Area   States in square units the area selected by a number of points.

Array (ar)   Creates **perpendicular** or **polar** arrays in 2D.

ASE   Provides links between AutoCAD and databases.

ASEadmin   Allows access to databases.

ASEexport   Exports data to databases.

ASElinks   Manipulates links between AutoCAD and databases.

ASErows   Edits links between AutoCAD and databases.

ASEselect   Creates links in rows between objects and databases.

ASEqled   Executes SQL (Structured Query Language).

Attdef   Allows editing of attributes from the Command Line.

Attedit   Allows editing of attributes from the Command Line.

Audit   Checks and fixes any errors in a drawing.

AutoSnap   Allows settings of **AutoSnap** features from the Command Line.

Bhatch (h or **bh)**   Brings the **Boundary Hatch** dialogue box on screen.

Blipmode   Sets blips on or off (1 or 0).

Block   Saves a drawing as a block within the same drawing.

Bmake (b)   Brings the **Block Definition** dialogue box on screen.

BMPout   Brings the **Create BMP File** dialogue box on screen.

Box   Creates a 3D solid box.

Boundary (bo)   Brings the **Boundary Creation** dialogue box on screen.

Break (br)   Breaks an object into parts.

Cal   For the calculation of mathematical expressions.

Calc   Brings the Windows 95 **Calculator** to screen.

Chamfer (cha)   Creates a chamfer between two entities.

Chprop (ch)   Changes properties of an entity through the **Change Properties** dialogue box.

Circle (c)   Creates a circle.

Cone   Creates a 3D model of a cone.

Copy (co)   Creates a single copy or multiple copies of selected entities.

Copy object (co)   The name of the **Copy** tool.

Copyclip (Ctrl+C)   Copies part of a drawing to the Windows 95 **Clipboard.**

Copylink   Forms a link between an AutoCAD drawing and its appearance in another application such as a word processing package.

Cylinder   Creates a 3D cylinder.

DBlist   Creates a database list in a text window for every entity in a drawing.

DDattdef (at)   Brings the **Attribute Definition** dialogue box on screen.

DDatte (ate)   Edits individual attribute values.

DDattext   Brings the **Attribute Extraction** dialogue box on screen.

DDchprop   Brings the **Change Properties** dialogue box on screen.

DDcolor (col)   Brings the **Select Color** dialogue box on screen.

DDedit (ed)   Select text and the **Edit Text** dialogue box appears.

DDgrips (gr)   Brings the **Grips** dialogue box on screen.

DDim   Brings the **Dimensions Styles** dialogue box on screen.

DDinsert (i)   Brings the **Insert** dialogue box on screen.

DDmodify (m)   Brings the **Modify** dialogue box for the selected entity on screen.

DDosnap (os)   Brings the **Osnap Settings** dialogue box on screen.

DDptype   Brings the **Point Style** dialogue box on screen.

DDrename   Brings the **Rename** dialogue box on screen.

DDrmodes (rm)   Brings the **Drawing Aids** dialogue box on screen.

DDselect (se)   Brings the **Object Selection Settings** dialogue box on screen.

DDucs (uc)   Brings the **UCS Control** dialogue box on screen.

DDucsp (ucp)   Brings the **UCS Orientation** dialogue box on screen.

DDunits (un)   Brings the **Units Control** dialogue box on screen.

DDview (v)   Brings the **View Control** dialogue box on screen.

DDvpoint (vp)   Brings the **Viewpoint Presets** dialogue box on screen.

Del   Allows a file (any file) to be deleted.

Dim   Starts a session of dimensioning.

Dim1   Allows the addition of a single addition of a dimension to a drawing.

There are a large number of set variables controlling methods of dimensioning. These are not included here.

Dish   Creates a 3D dish surface.

Dist (di)   Measures the distance between two points in coordinate units.

Divide (div)   Divides and entity into equal parts.

Dome   Creates a 3D dome surface.

Donut (do)   Creates a donut.

DSviewer   Brings the **Aerial View** window on screen.

Dtext (dt) Creates dynamic text. Text appears in drawing area as it is entered.

Dview (dv)   Instigates the dynamic view prompts sequence.

DXfout   Brings the **Create DXF File** dialogue box on screen.

DXfin   Brings the **Select DXF File** dialogue box on screen.

Edgesurf   Creates a 3D mesh surface from four adjoining edges.

Edit polyline (pe)   For the editing of polylines (plines).

Ellipse (el)   Creates an ellipse.

End   Finishes a drawing session and closes AutoCAD down.

Erase (e)   Erases selected entities from a drawing.

Exit   Ends a drawing session and closes AutoCAD down.

Explode (x)   Explodes a block or group into its various entities.

Explorer   Brings the Windows 95 Explorer on screen.

Export (exp)   Brings the **Export Data** dialogue box on screen.

Extend (ex)   To extend an entity to another.

Extrude (ext)   Extrudes a closed polyline into a 3D solid.

Fillet (f)   Creates a fillet between two entities.

Filter   Brings the **Object Selection Filters** dialogue box on screen.

Group (g)   Brings the **Object Grouping** dialogue box on screen.

Hatch   Allows hatching through responses to prompts.

Hatchedit (he)   Brings the **Hatchedit** dialogue box on screen.

Help   Brings the **Help Topics** dialogue box on screen.

Hide (hi)   To hide hidden lines in 3D models.

Id   Identifies a point on screen in coordinate units.

Imageadjust (iad)   Brings the **Image Adjust** dialogue box on screen.

Imageattach (iat)   Brings the **Image Attach File** dialogue box on screen.

Imageclip (iim)   Brings the **Image** dialogue box on screen.

Import (im)   Brings the **Import File** dialogue box on screen.

Insert (i)   Allows the insertion of a block by response to prompts at the Command Line.

Insertobj (ins)   Brings the **Insert Object** dialogue box.

Interfere (in)   Creates an interference solid from selection of several solids.

Intersect (int)   Creates an interference solid from a group of two or more solids.

Isoplane   Sets the isoplane when constructing an isometric drawing.

Layer (la)   Brings the **Layer and Linetype** dialogue box on screen.

Lengthen (len)   Lengthens an entity on screen.

Light   Brings the **Lights** dialogue box on screen.

Limits   Sets the drawing limits in coordinate units.

Line (l)   Creates a line.

Linetype (lt)   Brings the **Layer and Linetype** dialogue box on screen.

List (li)   Lists in an text window details of any entity or group of entities selected.

Load   Brings the **Select Drawing File** dialogue box on screen.

Logfileoff   The Text window contents are no longer recorded.

Logfileon   The Text window contents are recorded.

Ltscale (lts)   Allows the linetype scale to be adjusted.

Matchprop (ma)   Brings the **Property Settings** dialogue box on screen.

Matlib   Brings the **Materials Library** dialogue box on screen.

Measure (me)   Allows measured intervals to be placed along entities.

Menu   Brings the **Select Menu File** dialogue box on screen.

Menuload   Brings the **Menu Customization** dialogue box on screen.

Mirror (mi)   Creates an identical mirror image to selected entities.

Mirror3D   Mirrors 3D models in 3D space in selected directions.

Mledit   Brings the **Multiline Edit Tools** dialogue box on screen.

Mline (ml)   Creates mlines.

Mlstyle   Brings the **Multiline Styles** dialogue box on screen.

Move (m)   Allows selected entities to be moved.

Mslide   Brings the **Create Slide File** dialogue box on screen.

Mspace (ms)   Changes from Paperspace to Modelspace.

Mtext (mt or **t)**   Brings the **Multiline Text Editor** on screen.

Mview (mv)   When in PSpace brings in MSpace objects.

Mvsetup   Allows drawing specifications to be set up.

New (Ctrl+N)   Brings the **Create New Drawing** dialogue box on screen.

Notepad   Brings the Windows 95 **Notepad** on screen.

Offset (o)   Offsets selected entity by a stated distance.

Oops   Cancels the effect of using **Erase** and brings back a drawing after **WBlock.**

Open   Brings the **Select File** dialogue box on screen.

Ortho   Allows ortho to be toggled on or off.

Osnap (os)   Brings the **Osnap Settings** dialogue box on screen.

Pan (p)   Pans the R14 drawing editor in any direction.

Pasteclip (Ctrl+V)   Pastes a bitmap from the **Clipboard** into the drawing area.

Pastespec (pa)   Brings the **Paste Special** dialogue box on screen.

Pbrush   Brings Windows 95 **Paint** on screen.

Pedit (pe)   Allows editing of polylines.

Pface   Allows the construction of a 3D mesh through a number of selected vertices.

Plan   Allows a drawing in 3D space to be seen in plan (UCS World).

Pline (pl)   Creates a polyline.

Plot (ctrl+p)   Brings the **Plot/Print Configuration** dialogue box on screen.

Point (po)   Allows a point to be placed on screen.

Polygon (pol)   Creates a polygon.

Polyline (pl)   Creates a polyline.

Preferences (pr)   Brings the **Preferences** dialogue box on screen.

Preview (pre)   Brings the print/plot preview box on screen.

Print (ctrl+p)   Brings the **Plot/Print Configuration** dialogue box on screen.

PSfill   Allows polylines to be filled with patterns.

PSin   Brings the **Select Postscript File** dialogue box on screen.

PSout   Brings the **Create Postscript File** dialogue box on screen.

PSpace (ps)   Changes Modelspace to Paperspace.

Purge (pu)   Purges unwanted data from a drawing before saving to file.

Pyramid   Creates a 3D surface pyramid.

Qsave   Quicksave. Saves the drawing file to its current name.

Quit (q)   Ends a drawing session and closes down AutoCAD.

Ray   A construction line from a point and (usually) at an angle.

Reconfig   Reconfigures the setup for rendering.

Recover   Brings the **Select File** dialogue box on screen to allow recovery of selected drawings as necessary.

Rectang (rec)   Creates a pline rectangle.

Redefine   If an AutoCAD Command name has been turned off by **Undefine**, turns the command name back on.

Redo   Cancels the last **Undo.**

Redraw (r)   Redraws the contents of the R14 drawing area.

Redrawall (ra)   Redraws the whole of a drawing.

Regen (re)   Regenerates the contents of the R14 drawing area.

Regenall (rea)   Regenerates the whole of a drawing.

Region (reg)   Creates a region from an area within a boundary.

Rename (ren)   Brings the **Rename** dialogue box on screen.

Render (rre)   Brings the **Render** dialogue box on screen.

Replay   Brings the **Replay** dialogue box on screen from which bitmap image files can be selected.

Revolve (rev)   Forms a solid of revolution from outlines.

Revsurf   Creates a solid of revolution from a pline.

Rmat   Brings the **Materials** dialogue box on screen.

Rotate (ro)   Rotates selected entities around a selected point.

Rotate3D   Rotates a 3D model in 3D space in all directions.

Rpref (rpr)   Brings the **Rendering Preferences** dialogue box on screen.

Rulesurf   Creates a 3D mesh between two entities.

Save (Ctrl+S)   Brings the **Save Drawing As** dialogue box on screen.

Saveas (save)   Brings the **Save Drawing As** dialogue box on screen.

Saveasr12   Allows a drawing to be saved in Release 12 drawing file format.

Saveimg   Brings the **Save Image** dialogue box on screen.

Scale (sc)   Allows selected entities to be scaled in size – smaller or larger.

Scene   Brings the **Scene** dialogue box on screen.

Script (scr)   Brings the **Select Script File** dialogue box on screen.

Section (sec)   Creates a section plane in a 3D model.

Setvar (set)   Can be used to bring a list of the settings of set variables into an AutoCAD Text window.

Shade (sha)   Shades a selected 3D model.

Shape   Inserts an already loaded shape into a drawing.

Shell   Allows MS-DOS commands to be entered.

Sketch   Allows freehand sketching.

Slice (sl)   Allows a 3D model to be cut into two parts.

Solid (so)   Creates a filled outline in triangular parts.
Solprof   Creates a profile from a 3D solid model drawing.
Spell (sp)   Brings the **Check Spelling** dialogue box on screen.
Sphere   Creates a 3D solid surface sphere.
Spline (spl)   Creates a spline curve through selected points.
Splinedit (spe)   Allows the editing of a spline curve.
Stats   Brings the **Statistics** dialogue box on screen.
Status   Shows the status (particularly memory use) in a Text window.
Stlout   Saves a 3D model drawing in ASCII or binary format.
Stretch (s)   Allows selected entities to be stretched.
Style (st)   Brings the **Text Styles** dialogue box on screen.
Subtract (su)   Subtracts one 3D solid from another.
Tablet (ta)   Allows a tablet to be used with a pointing device.
Tabsurf   Creates a 3D solid from an outline and a direction vector.
Tbconfig   Brings the **Toolbars** dialogue box on screen to allow configuration of a toolbar.
Text (dt)   Allows text from the Command Line to be entered into a drawing.
Textqulty   Sets the resolution for printing TrueType text for plotting.
Thickness (th)   Sets the thickness for the Elevation command.
Tolerance (to)   Brings the **Symbol** dialogue box on screen from which geometric tolerance symbols can be selected.
Toolbar (to)   Brings the **Toolbars** dialogue box on screen.
Torus (tor)   Allows a 3D torus to be created.
Trim (tr)   Allows entities to be trimmed up to other entities.
Type   Types the contents of a named file to screen.
Undefine   Suppresses an AutoCAD command name.
Undo (u) (Ctrl+Z)   Undoes the last action of a tool.
Union (uni)   Unites 3D solids into a single solid.
Un   Brings the **Units Control** dialogue box on screen. Allows setting of units by *entering* figures in a text window.
UCSfollow   The variable which when 'on' (1), allows UCS planes to be set.
View   Allows a view to be controlled – deleted, restored or saved.
Vplayer   Controls the visibility of layers in Paperspace.
Vpoint   Allows viewing positions to be set by *x,y,z* entries.
Vports   Allows viewport settings to be made.
Vslide   Brings the **Select Slide File** dialogue box on screen.
Wblock (w)   Brings the **Create Drawing File** dialogue box on screen.
Wedge (we)   Creates a 3D solid in the shape of a wedge.
WMFin   Brings the **Import WMF File** dialogue box on screen.
WMFopts   Brings the **Import Options** dialogue box on screen.
WMFout   Brings the **Create WMF** dialogue box on screen.
Xattach (xa)   Brings the **Select file to attach** dialogue box on screen.
Xline   Creates a construction line.
Xref (xr)   Brings the **External Reference** dialogue box on screen.
Zoom (z)   Brings the **Zoom** tool into action.

Index

PRINCESSES wear Trainers

To my husband Ben and our little girls Imogen and Elle.

First published in Great Britain in 2022
by Little Steps Publishing
Uncommon, 126 New King's Rd, London SW6 4LZ
www.littlestepspublishing.co.uk

ISBN: 978-1-912678-62-4

A CIP catalogue record for this book is available from the British Library.

Designed by Nina Nielsen and Malinda Hadiwidjojo
Printed in China
1 3 5 7 9 10 8 6 4 2